AF544941

BARNABY FURNAS
FLOODS

With essays by Nora Burnett Abrams and Adam Lerner

MUSEUM OF CONTEMPORARY ART DENVER

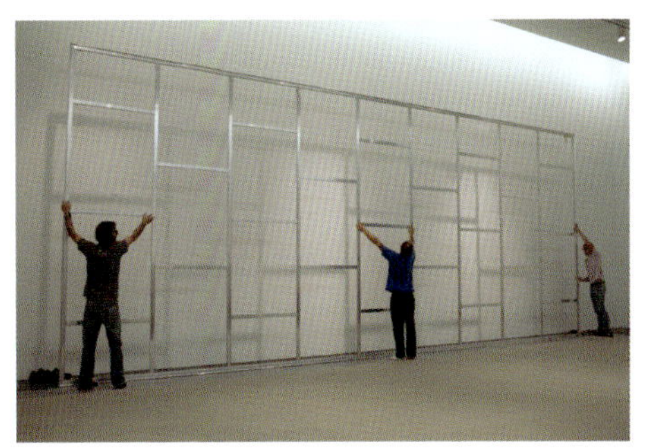

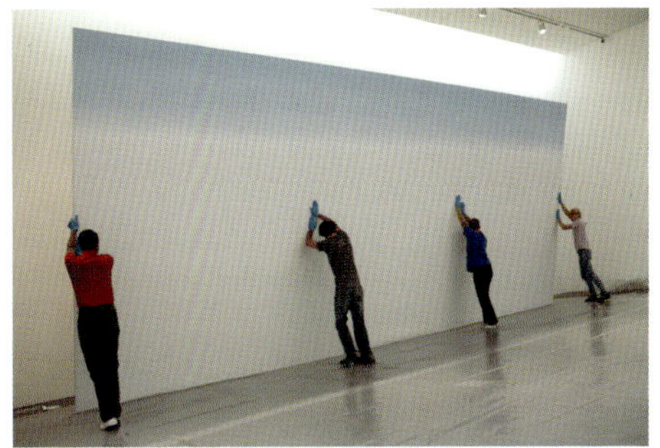

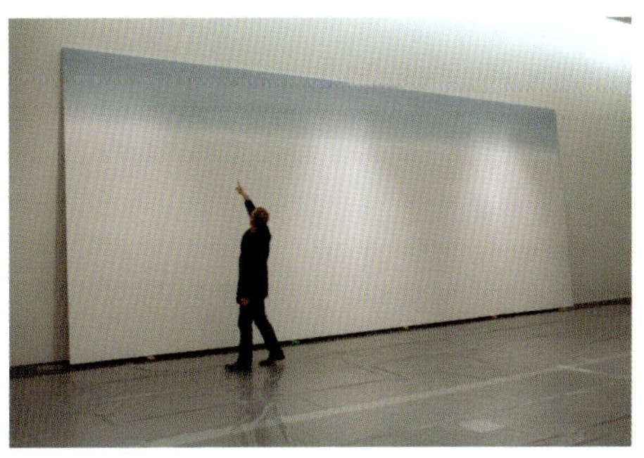

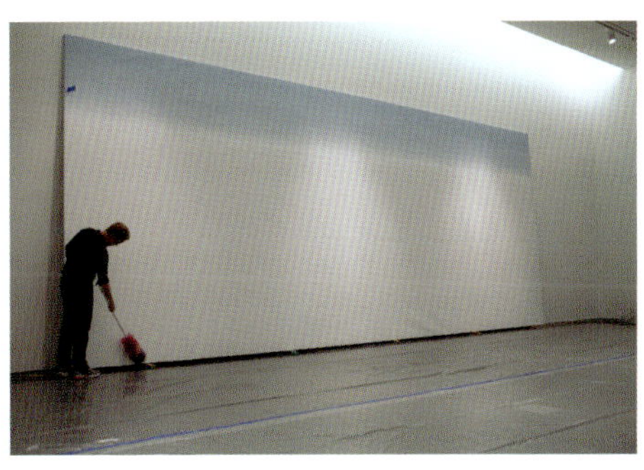

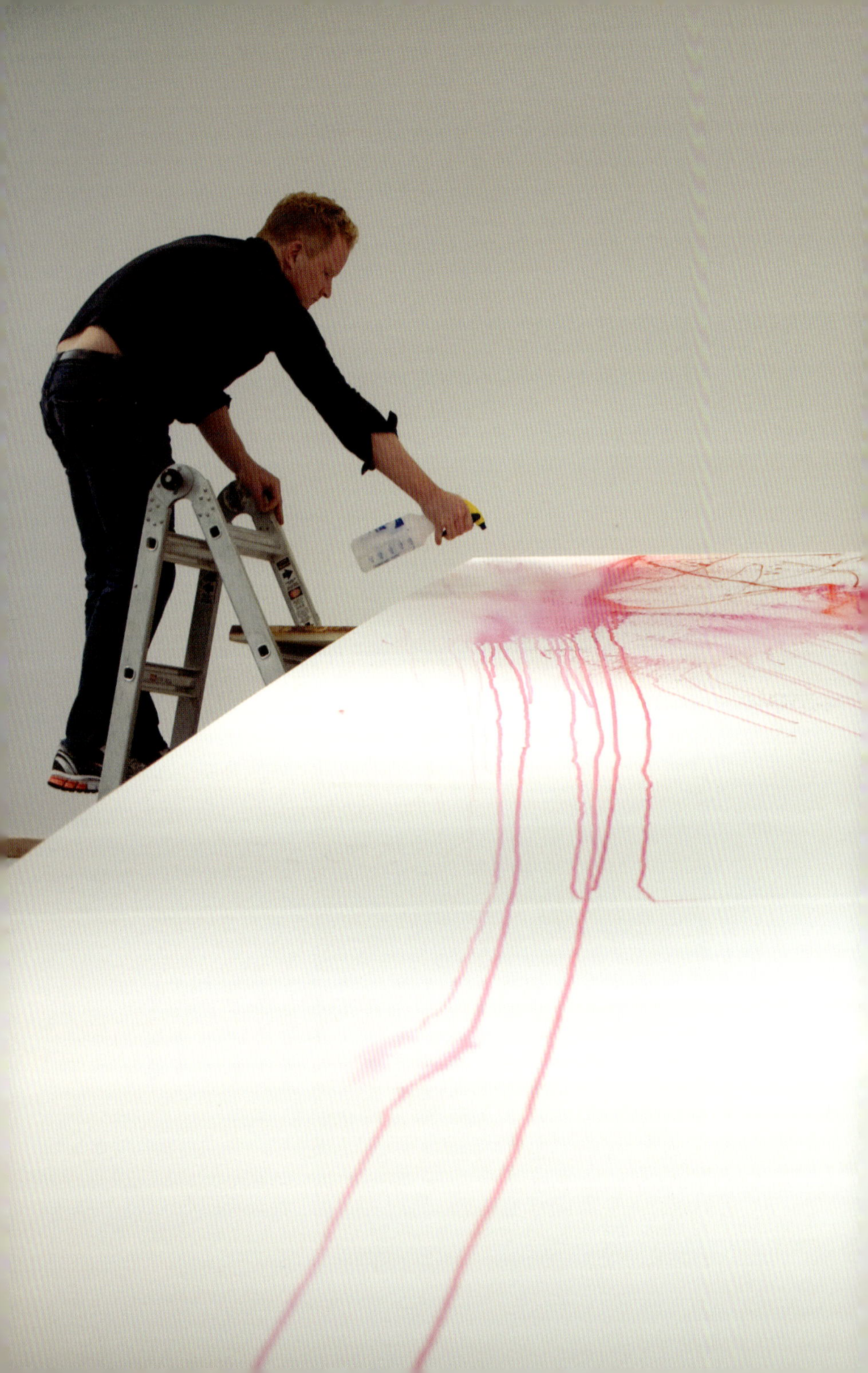

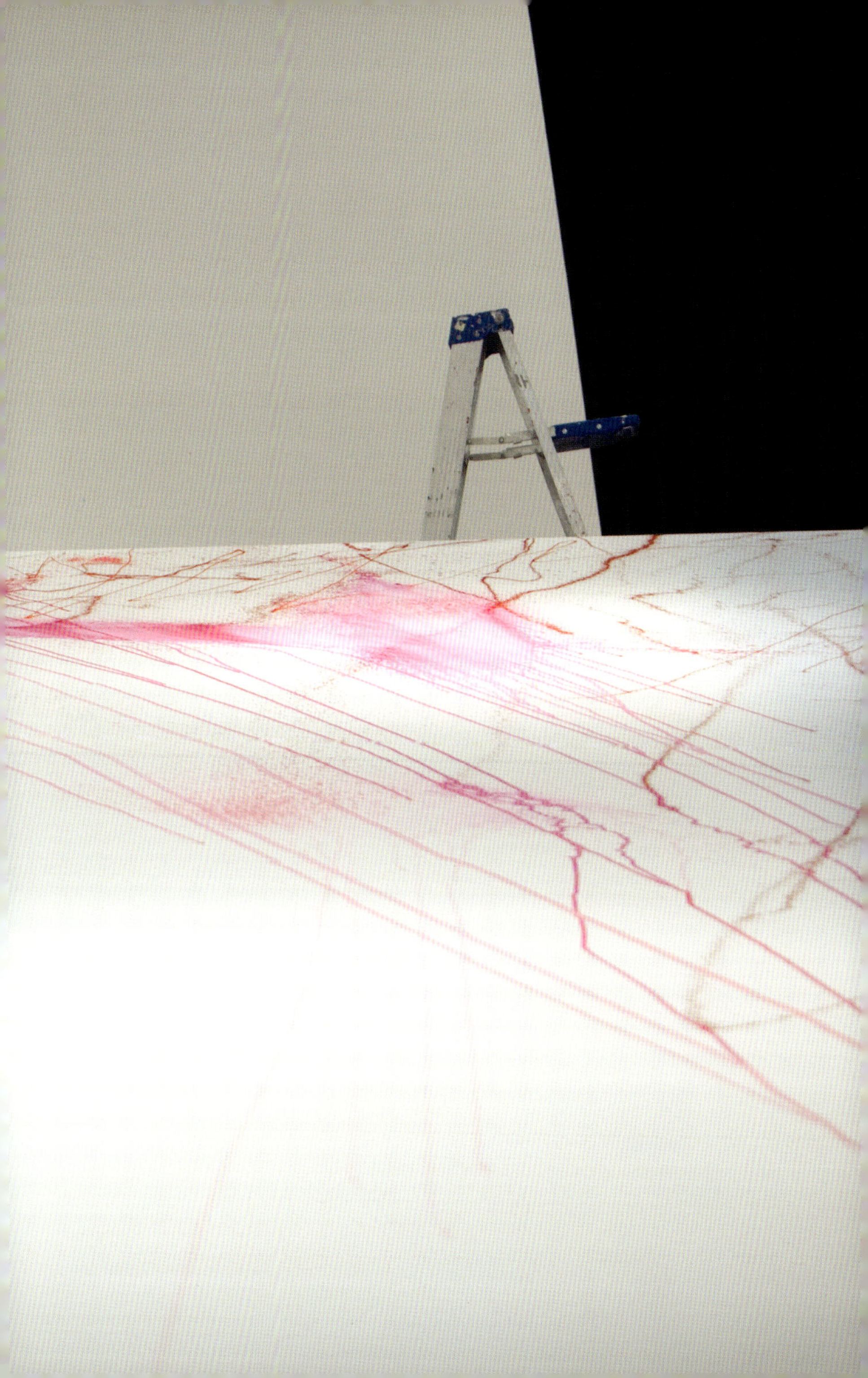

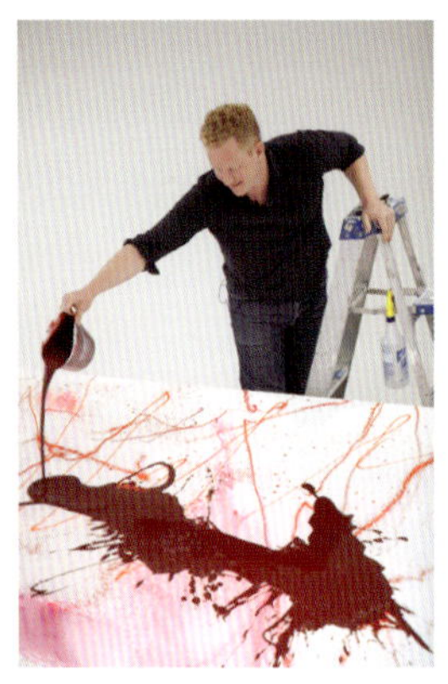

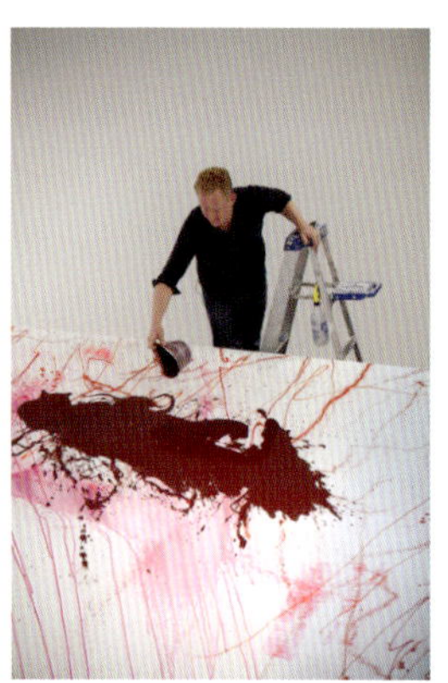

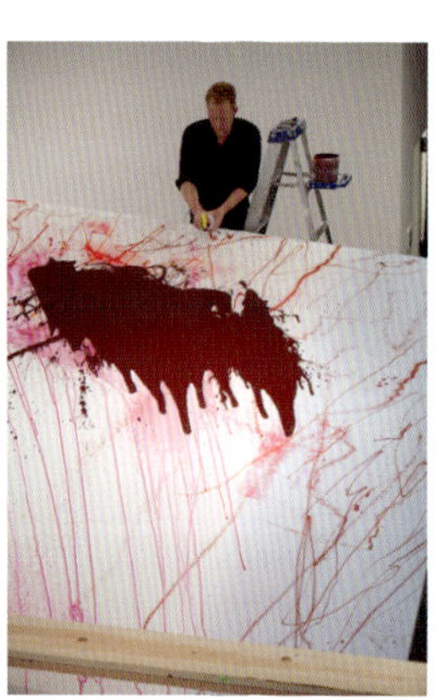

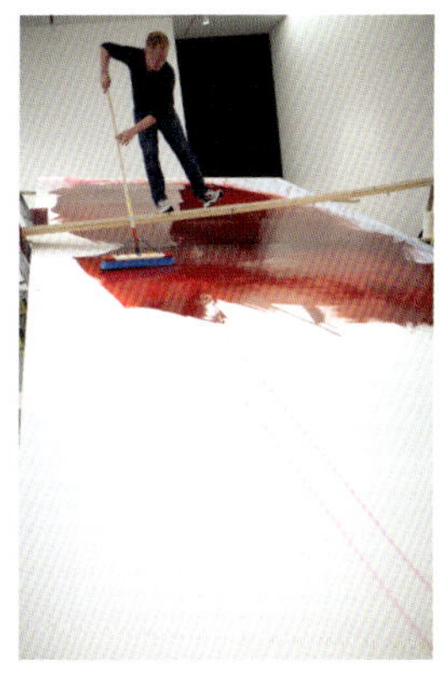
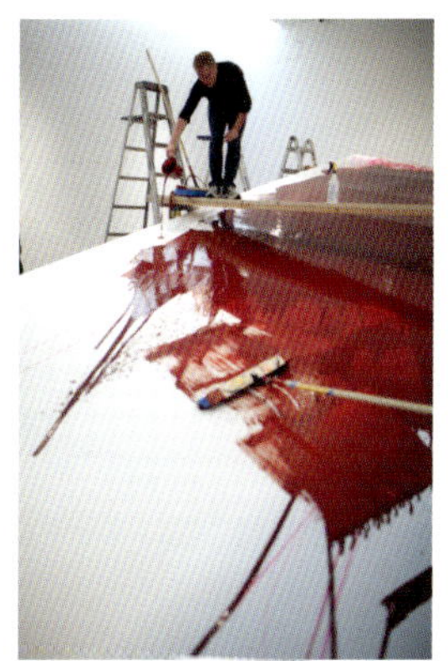
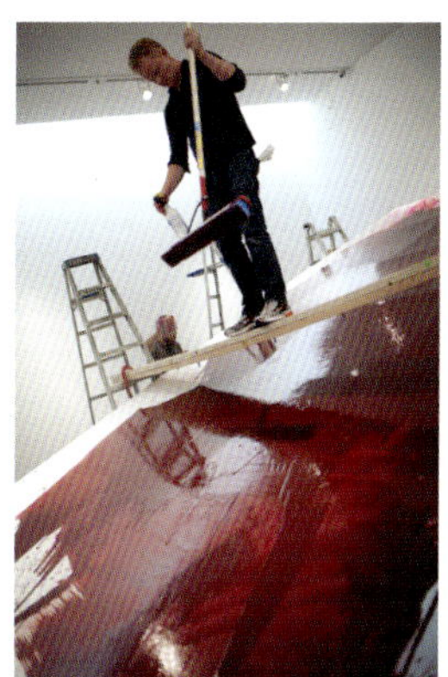

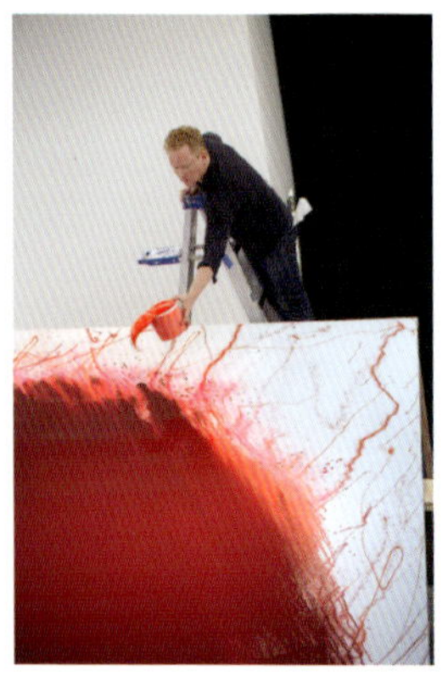

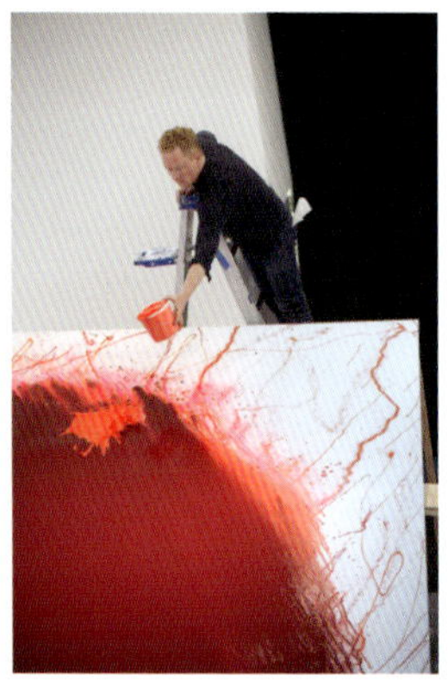

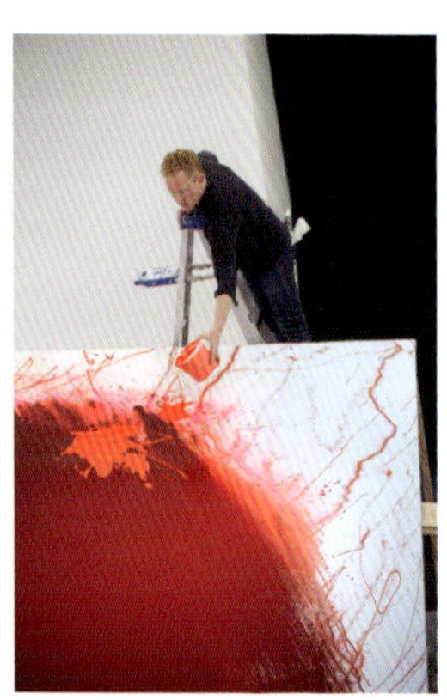

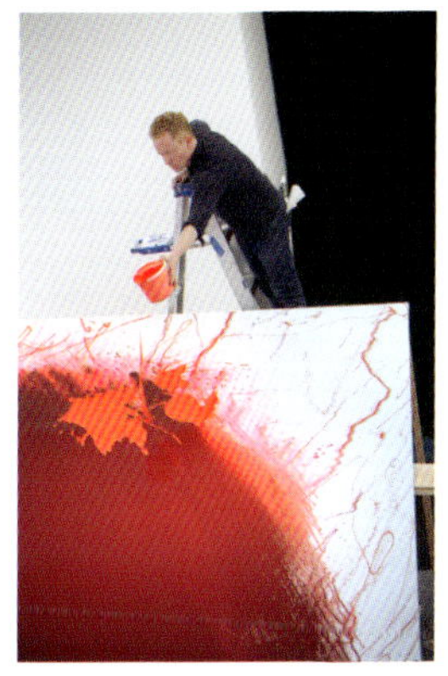
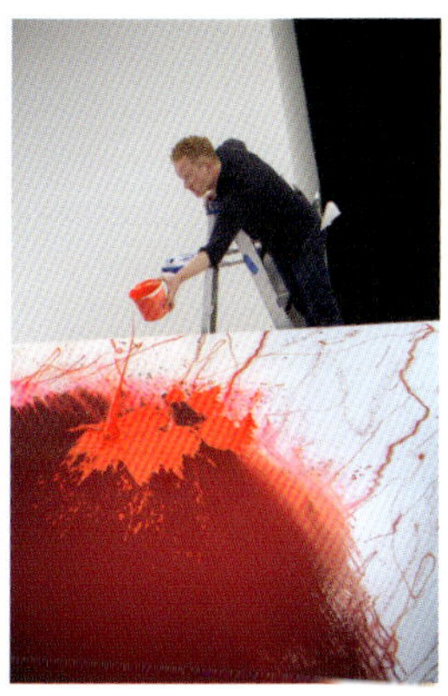
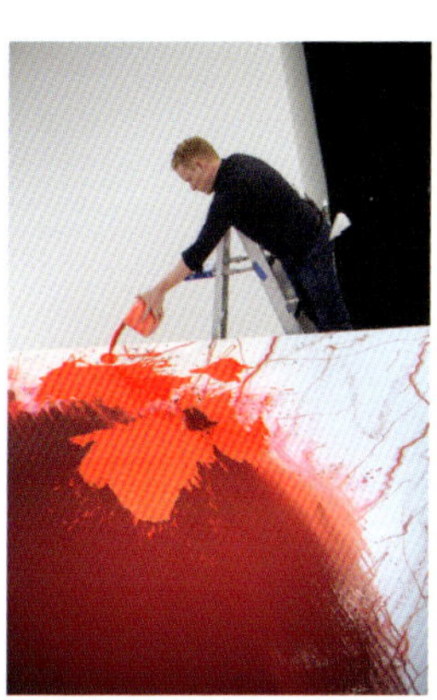

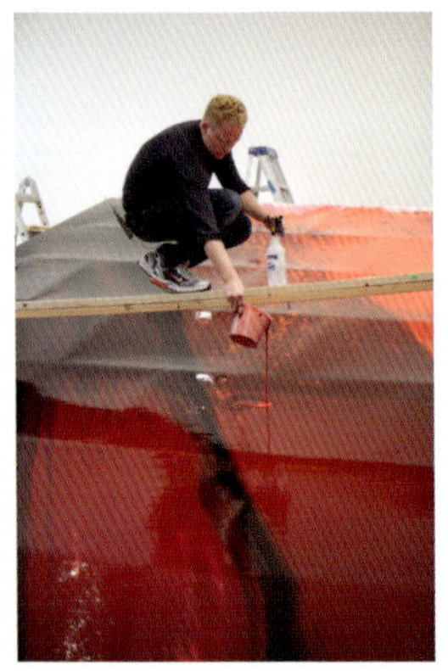

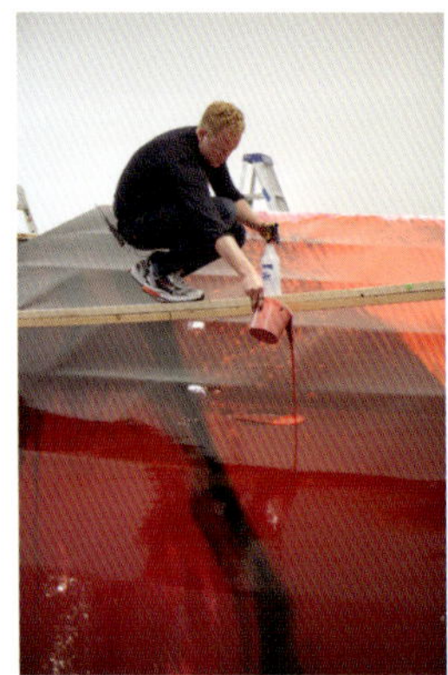

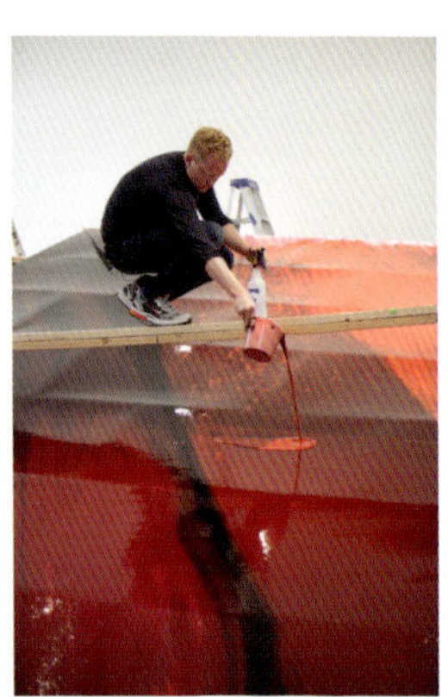

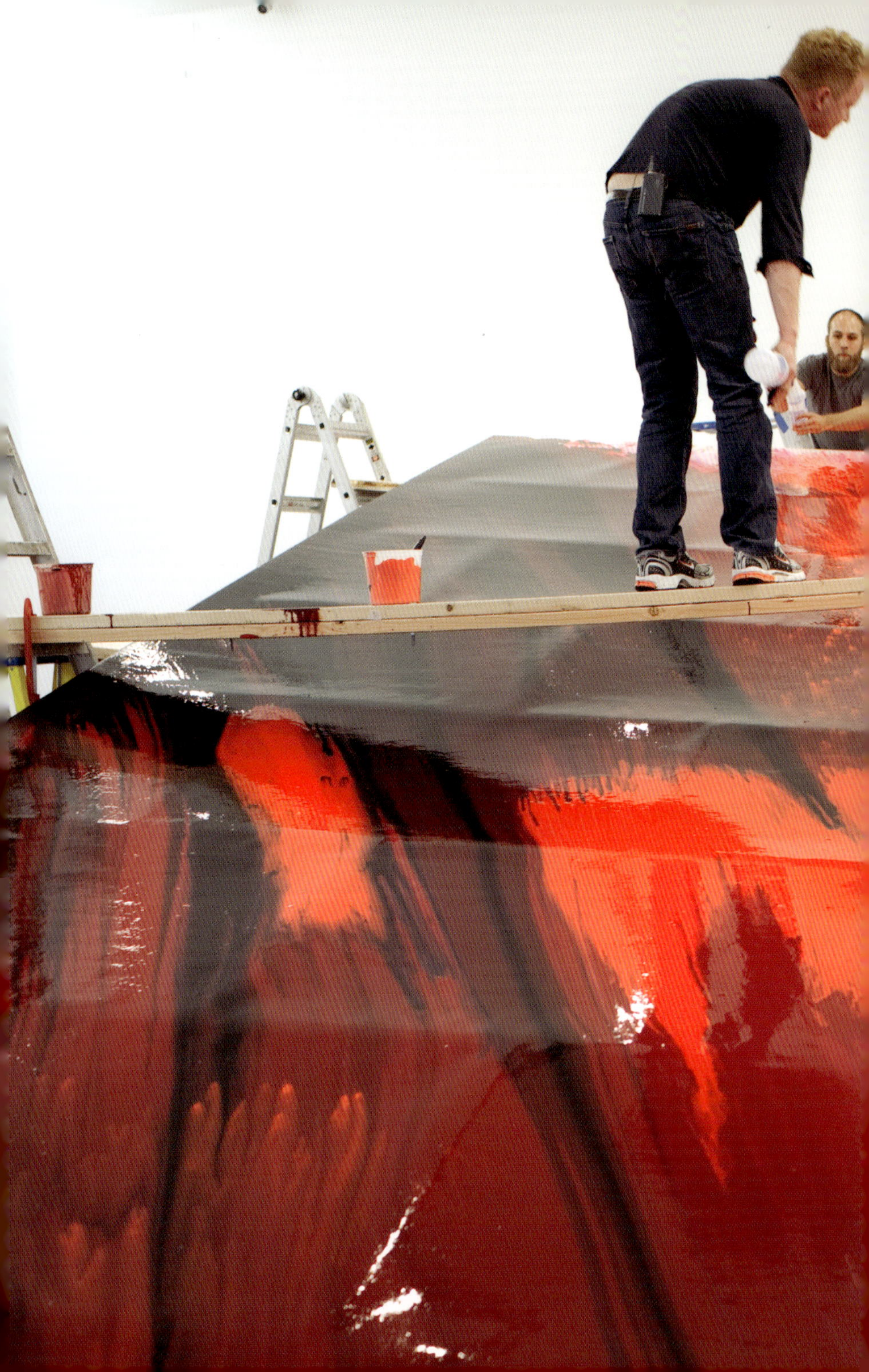

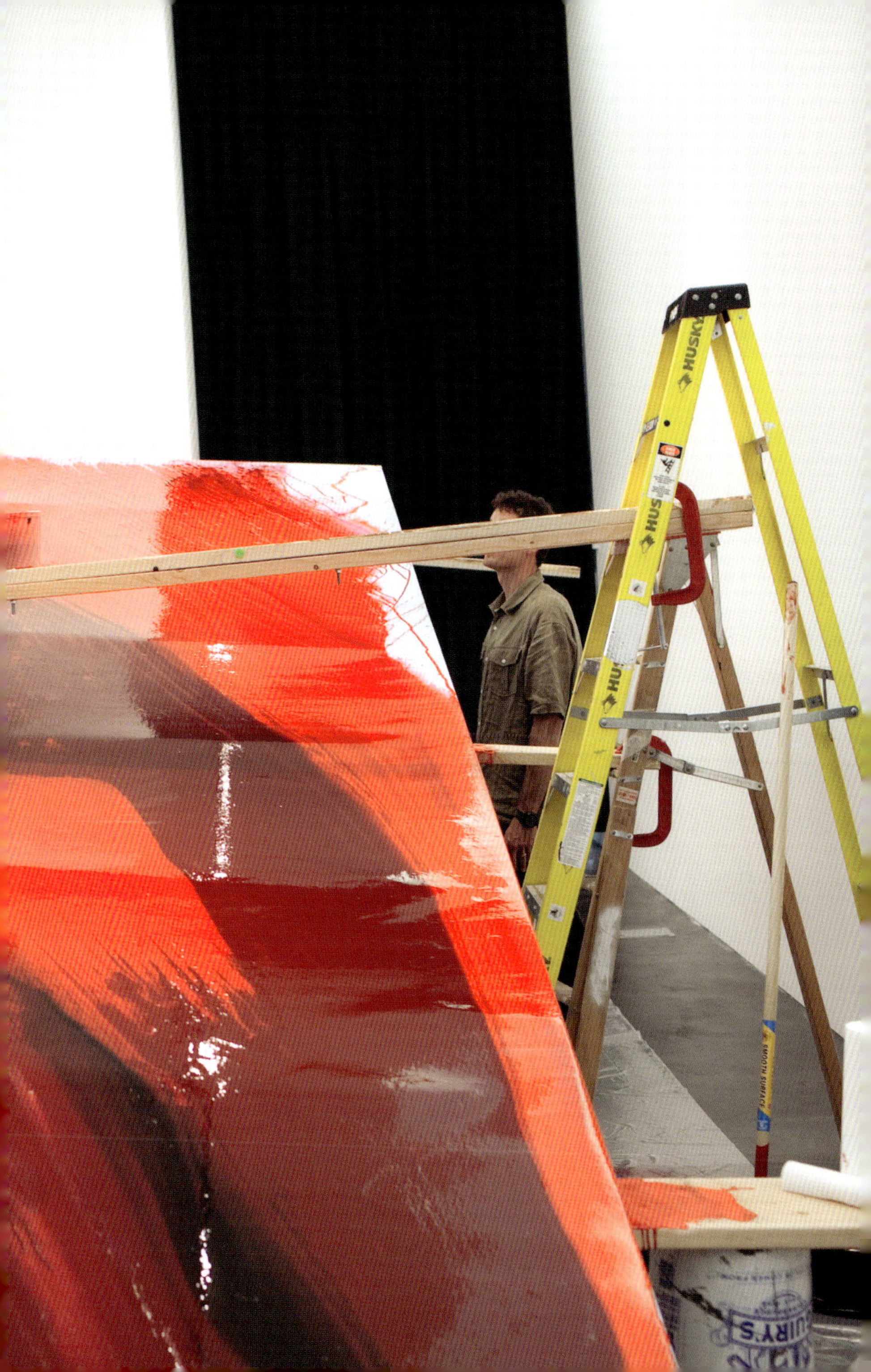

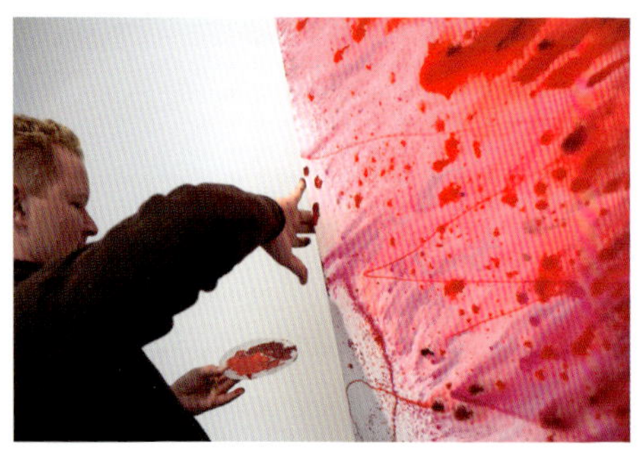

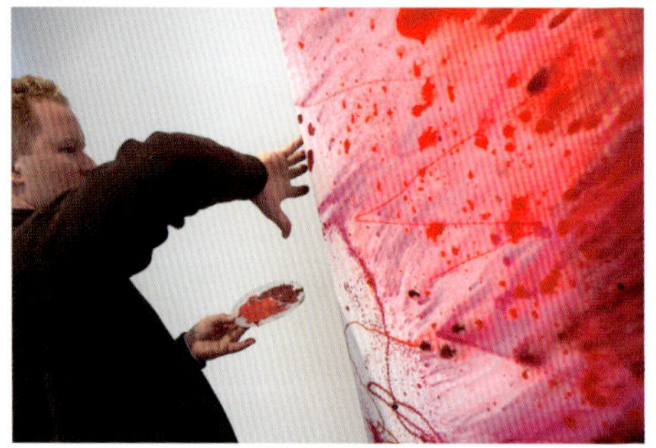

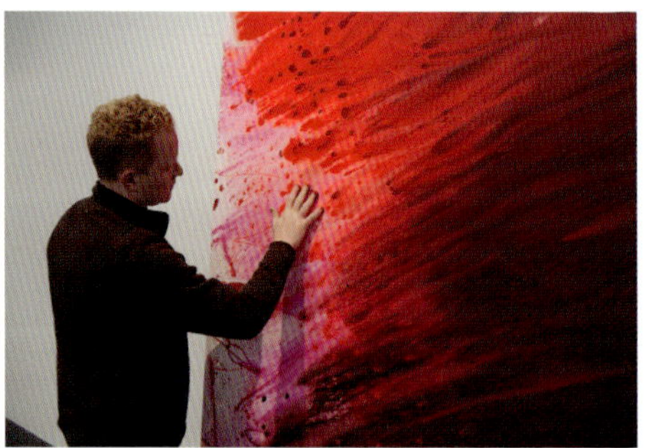

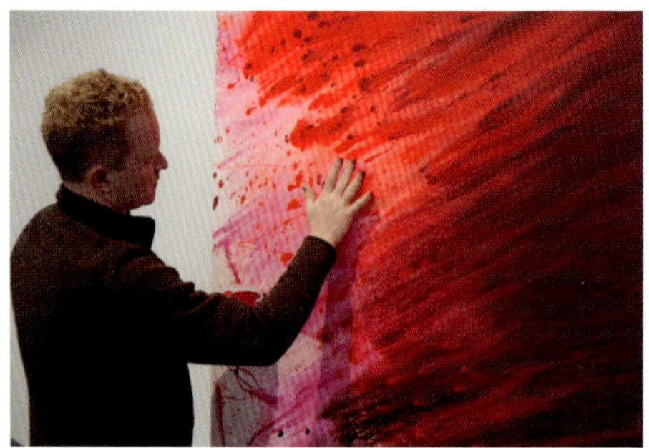

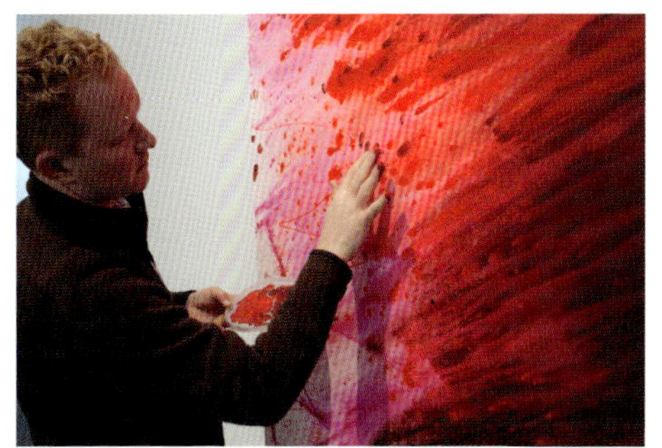

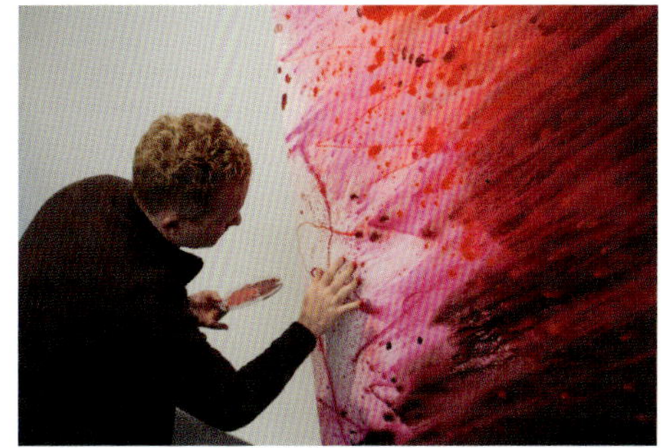

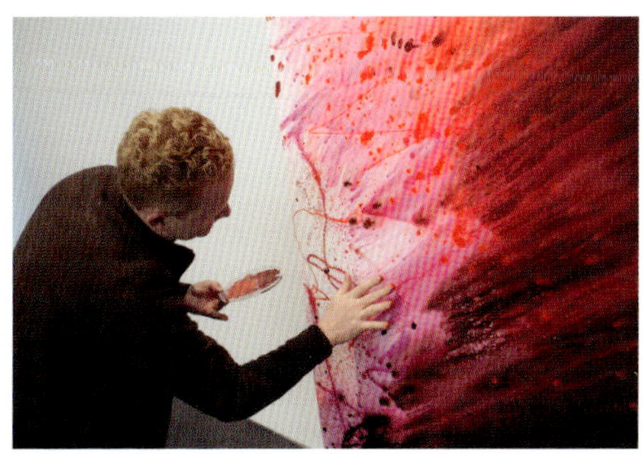

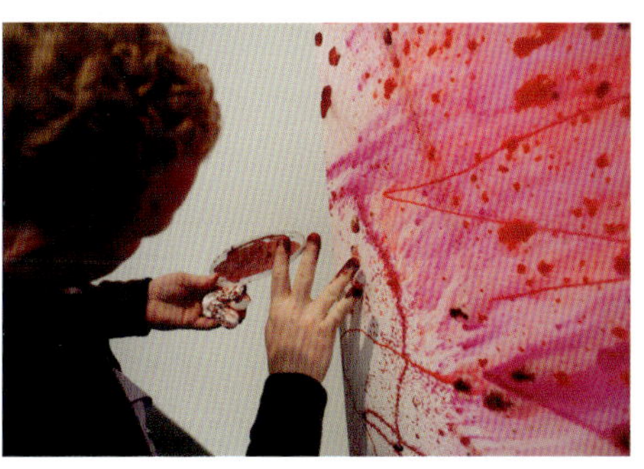

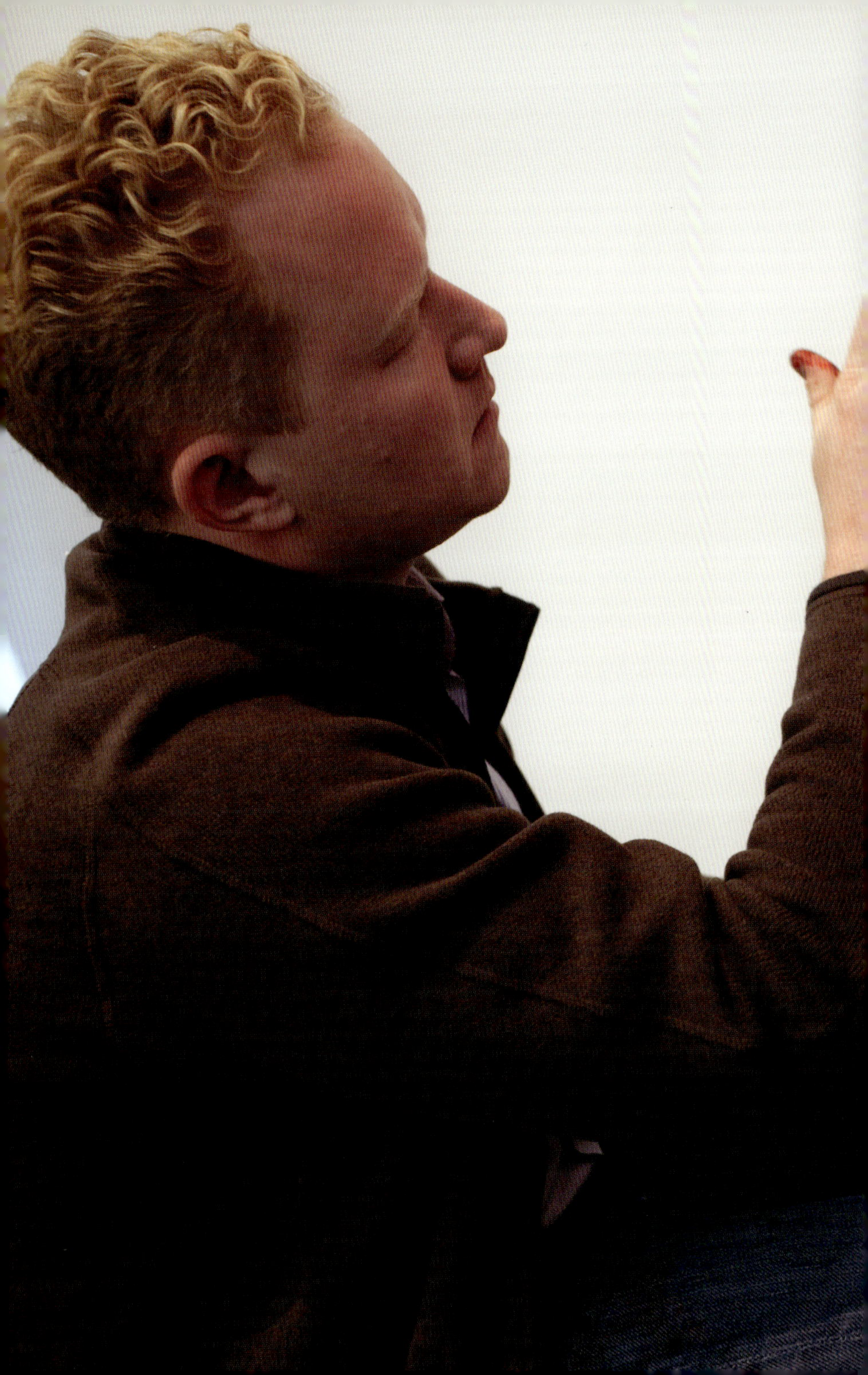

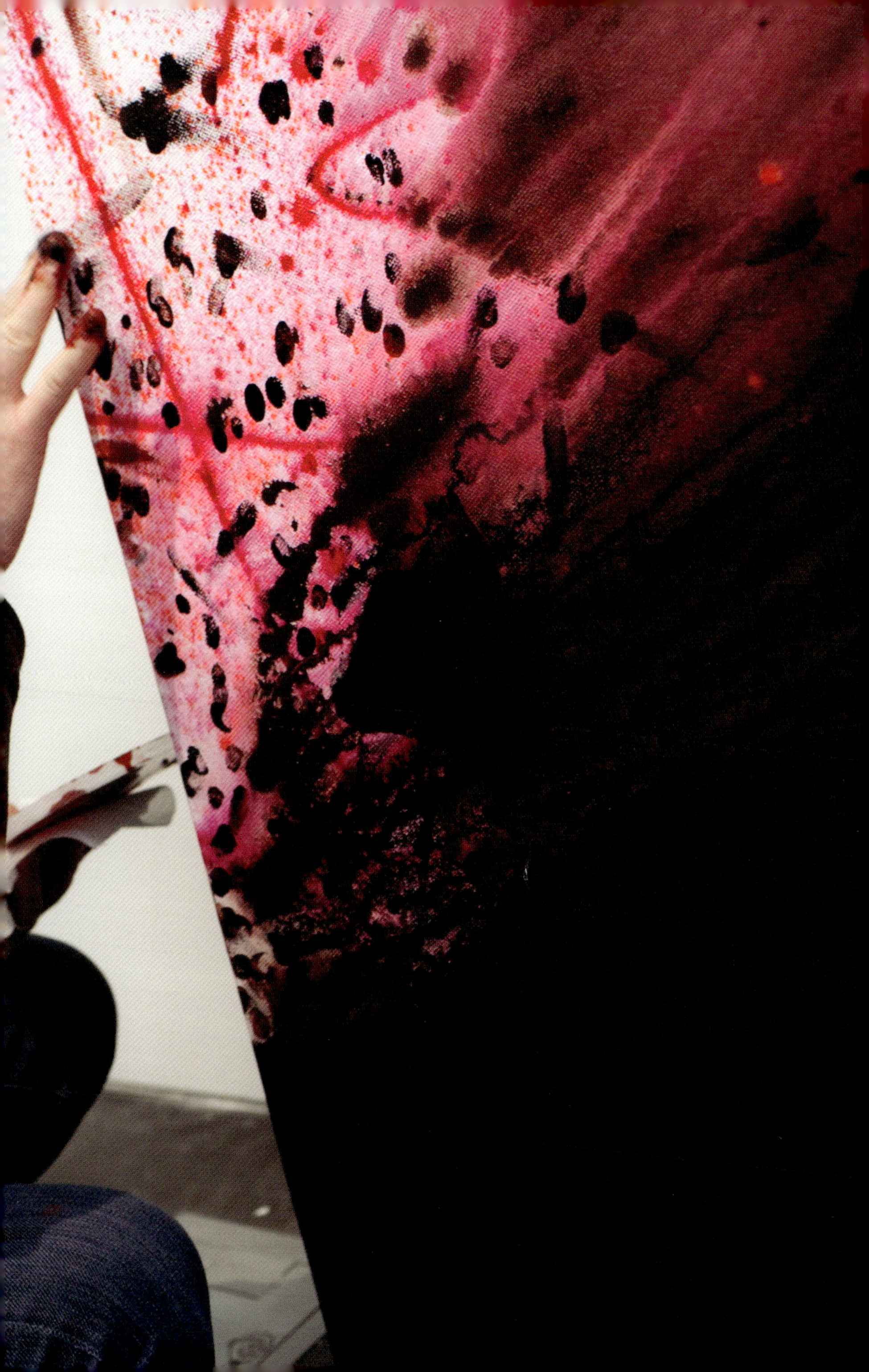

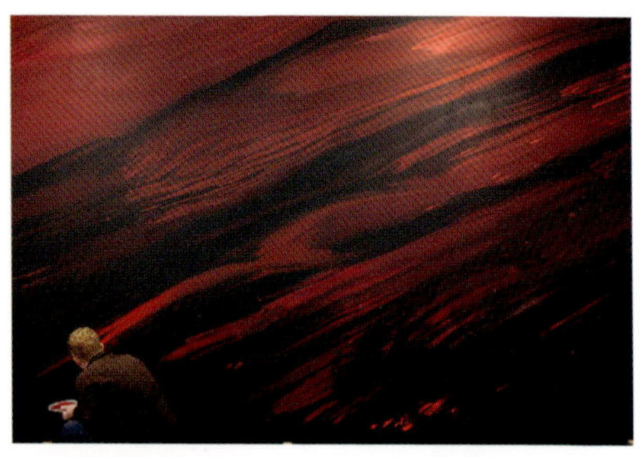

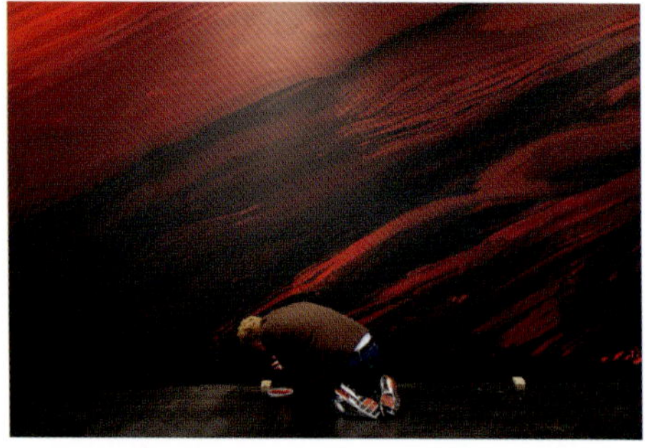

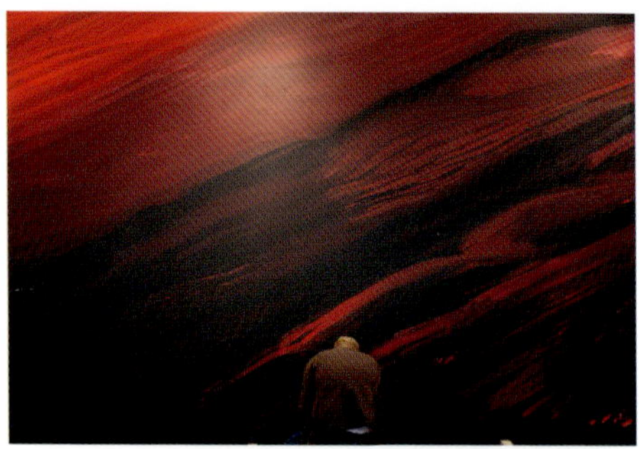

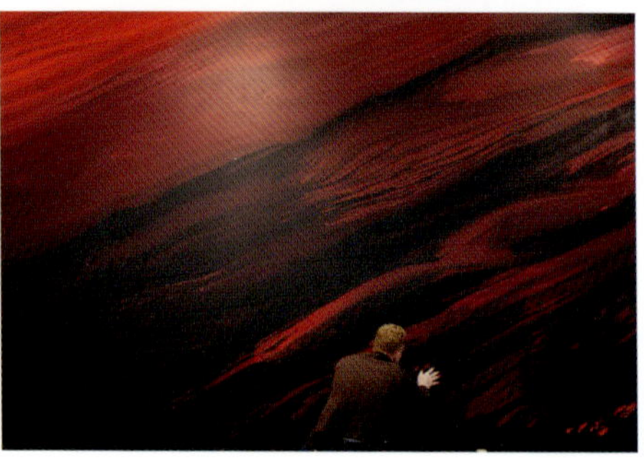

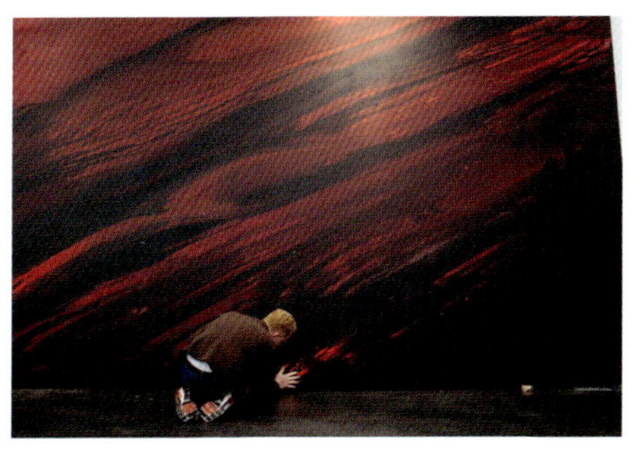

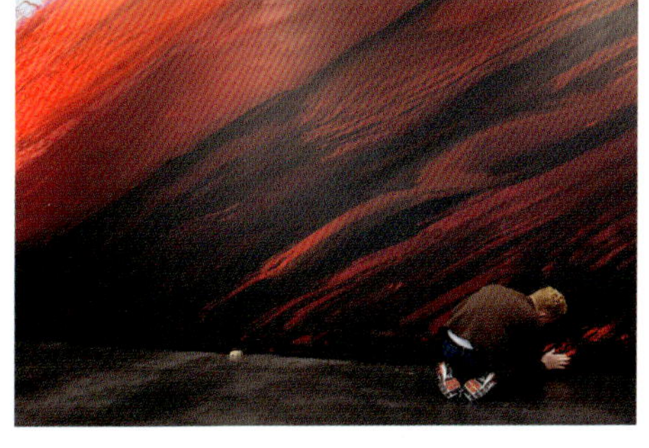

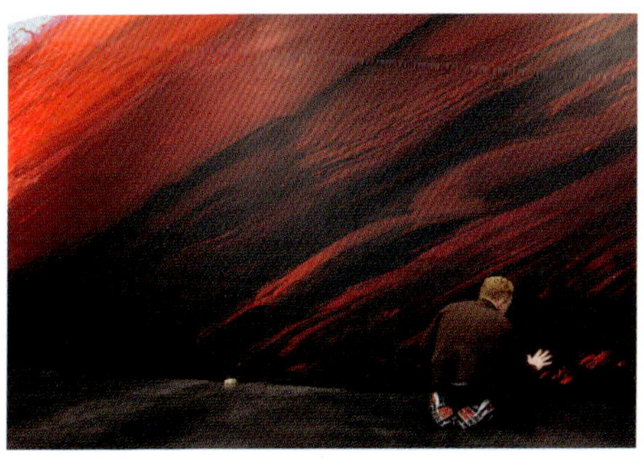

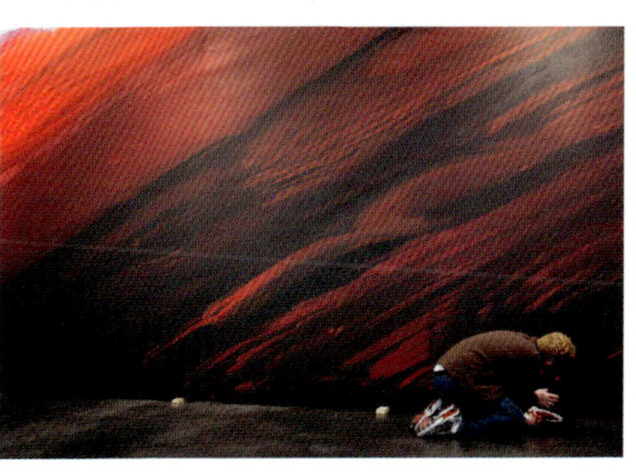

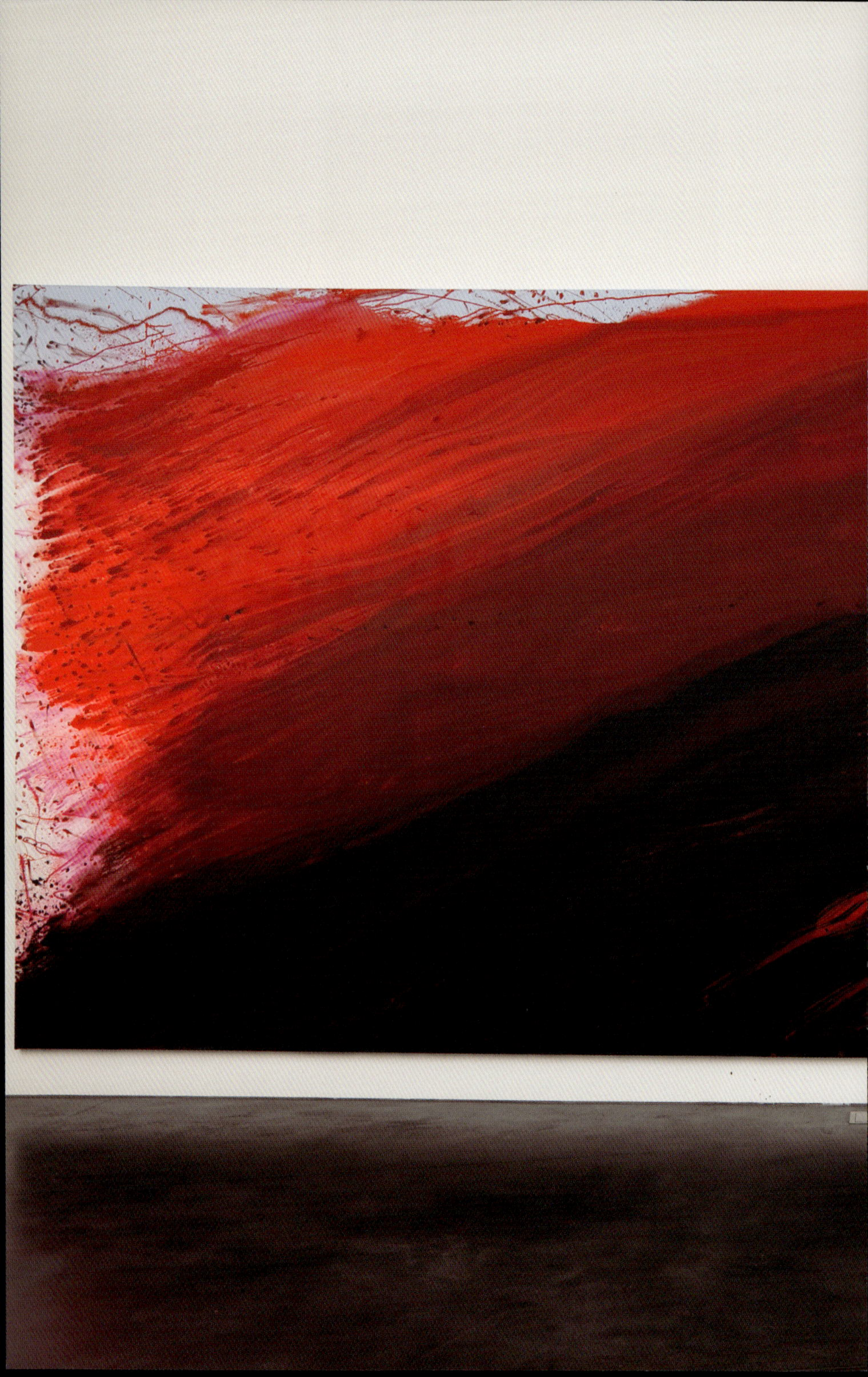

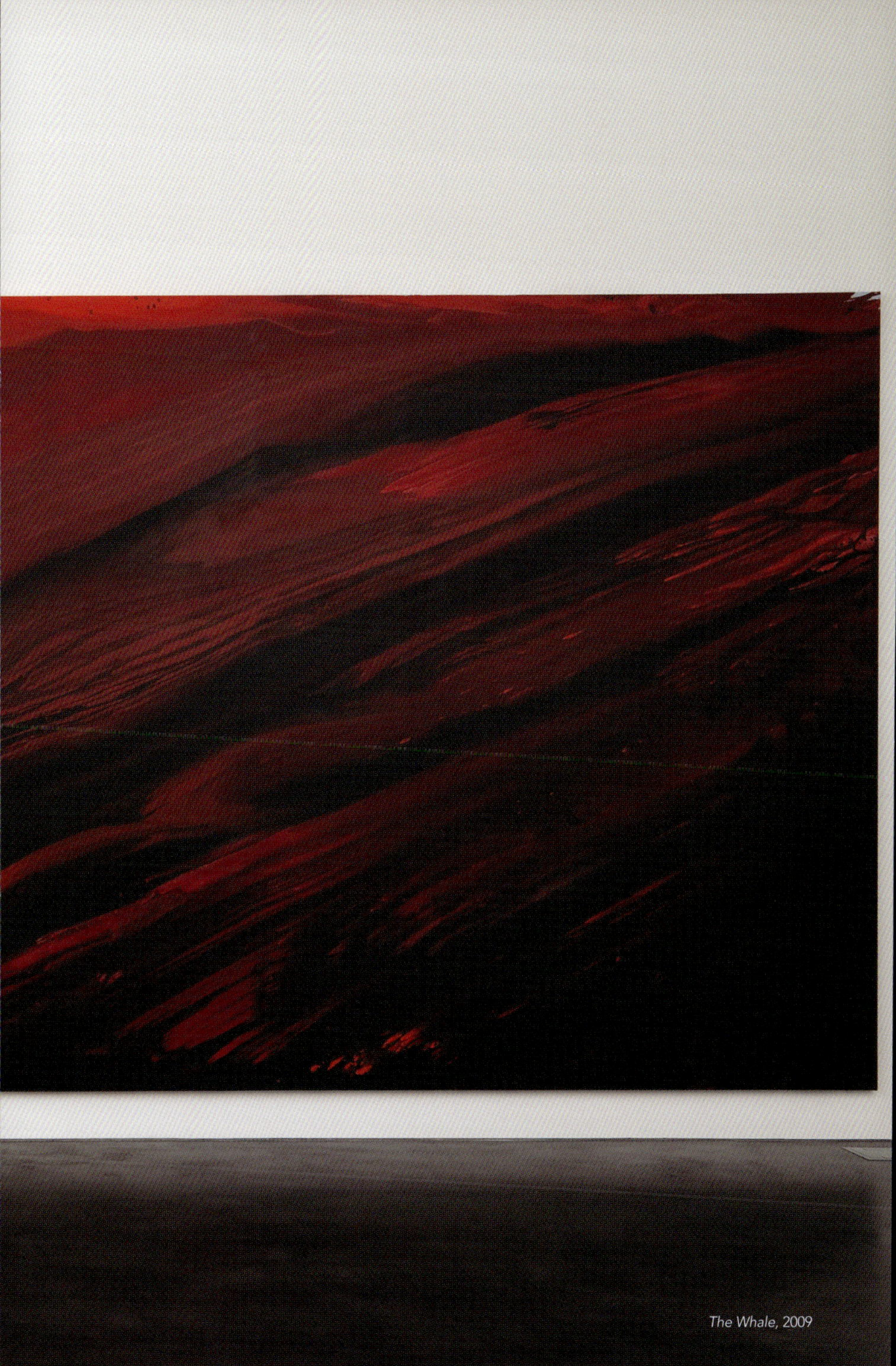

The Whale, 2009

BARNABY FURNAS AND BARNETT NEWMAN

BY NORA BURNETT ABRAMS

Floods, Barnaby Furnas's recent series of majestically scaled and boldly colored paintings, call to mind both biblical and contemporary events. The flood of Noah and his ark and the flood that drowned the Egyptians in the Red Sea are but two legendary examples, while the floods unleashed by Hurricane Katrina bring such mythic stories perilously into the present. Both natural disaster and brutal erasure, a flood envelops its victims, only to abandon them to ruins. And yet, in its destruction, a flood also generates new possibilities and offers that most elusive of desires: a second chance. In its wake, a flood introduces new prospects and new opportunities; it creates the inverse of its destruction by offering a new beginning.

An end and a beginning, the flood of Furnas's canvases obscures a tranquil landscape of light hues with aggressive stains of red acrylic, urethane and other water-based pigments—chosen precisely for how well they swim across the canvas and are absorbed by the fibers of the cotton. A flood's duality of erasure and possibility is manifested formally on the canvas, in the contrast between the poured red and the faint, zip-like vertical line that runs down the center of many of these paintings. This zip is a deliberate reference to the vertical strips of paint made famous by the

American Abstract Expressionist Barnett Newman (1905–1970) and his works, beginning in 1948. As is evident in *Abraham*, 1949, or *Vir Heroicus Sublimis*, 1950–1951, Newman's gesture simultaneously cleaved the canvas and opened it up, its simplicity belying an enormous effort to address the greatest of artistic challenges: the materialization of the sublime.

The sublime positions pleasure and fear as two sides of the same coin. For centuries, it has preoccupied philosophers, writers and artists seeking to codify encounters with the sublime in the unique conditions of their contemporary environments. A 19th-century Romantic painter like Caspar David Friedrich (German, 1774–1840) represented the sublime by presenting nature as an awesome sight—both fearful and marvelous, present though unknowable, factual and phenomenal, all at once. Often deploying a landscape of densely packed trees or craggy mountaintops, Friedrich offered nature as beautiful though haunting in its scale. To penetrate the massive forest or descend the mountainous terrain of his paintings is to set off on a path without the aid of reason or logic, and to surrender one's self to the unknown details that might exist within the depicted scene. The lone figures that populate his work serve as stand-ins for the viewer, by allowing us to situate ourselves within the painting and confront the complexity of emotions that these settings incite.

In the mid-20th century, however, the sublime meant something rather different for Newman. His challenge, departing from earlier representations *of* the sublime, was to make the act of painting *a sublime act*. Rather than describing the sublime, he articulated it, gave it a voice and set it in the present. In 1948 (the same year he produced his first zip painting), Newman published the essay "The Sublime is Now," clarifying his view that the sublime was no longer to be found in nature or in images of haunting beauty: The sublime emerged out of the individual artist's emotional condition—and was conditioned by him. He wrote:

We are freeing ourselves of the impediments of memory, association, nostalgia, legend, myth, or what have you, that have been the devices of Western European painting. Instead of making cathedrals out of Christ, man, or "life," we are making [them] out of ourselves, out of our own feelings. The image we produce is the self-evident one of revelation, real and concrete, that can be understood by anyone who will look at it without the nostalgic glasses of history.[1]

By shedding pictorial conventions such as narrative or figuration, and by shifting the focus of the sublime from an experience that occurred in the past to one that occurs in the present action of painting, Newman made the sublime an event.

As philosopher and critic Jean-Francois Lyotard has written of Newman's instantiation of the sublime, "...there is this painting where there might have been nothing at all, and that is the sublime. Letting go and disarming all grasping intelligence, recognizing that this occurrence of painting was not necessary...."[2] In this instance of Newman's painting, the sublime involves both anxiety (will he or can he make this painting?) and exaltation (making the painting) and never privileges one over the other. Newman's sublime is a constant state of both angst and euphoria, and is always set in the present. Lyotard even offered that Newman's essay should be translated from "The Sublime is Now" to "...'Now the Sublime is This'—not elsewhere, not up there or over there, not earlier or later...but here, now, 'it happens'—and it's this painting."[3]

1 Barnett Newman, "The Sublime is Now" in *Barnett Newman: Selected Writings and Interviews*. Edited by John P. O'Neill (New York: Alfred A. Knopf, 1990), 173.

2 Jean-Francois Lyotard, "The Sublime and the Avant-Garde," Artforum vol. 22 no. 8 (April 1984): 37.

3 Idem.

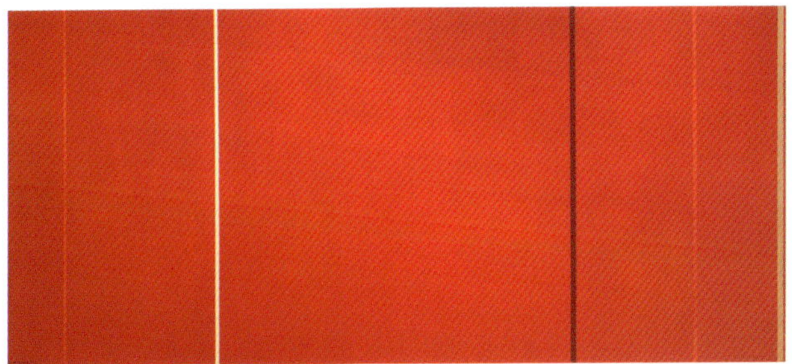

Figure 1 (above): Barnett Newman, *Vir Heroicus Sublimis*, 1950-51
Figure 2 (left): Barnett Newman, *Abraham*, 1949

With this insistence on and commitment to the present-ness of the sublime, Newman's focus was no longer on *what* was being painted in terms of figuration, abstraction, or even style, but rather on the compulsion to paint—as epitomized by his zips of paint bisecting the canvas. As Lyotard noted, Newman's application of the zip revealed a shift: He no longer desired for his work to imitate nature but instead for it to become "an artifact."[4] The final painting is, in the end, about presenting what is essentially un-presentable; Newman's gesture, no longer burdened by the task of mimesis, is bound ineluctably to what is not evident in nature.

Despite eschewing mimesis and illusionism, Newman never gave up subject matter. In order for his paintings to have meaning, they had to be about something and, ultimately, his subject in many ways became artistic creativity itself.[5] With titles ranging from *Abraham, Adam, Genesis—The Break* and other allusions to origins, an important focus of Newman's *oeuvre* was contending with creation and creative production.[6] Inasmuch as his definition of creation shifted during his career, both his creative ambitions and his subject matter were deeply entrenched in this desire to render a painting that denied the viewer any *a priori* references or meaning.[7] To view his painting was to encounter something heretofore unknown. For Newman, the sublime act was to introduce an experience of which the viewer had no prior understanding; to originate both stylistically and iconographically were two halves of a whole. His approach to creating a work meant making that work about the creative act, which was, of course, also the sublime act. Ultimately, with this focus on artistic creativity, we arrive at a state of promise, of possibility—we are at a new beginning.

4 Ibid, 41.

5 Jean-Francois Lyotard, "Newman: The Instant," in The Lyotard Reader. Ed. by Andrew Benjamin (Oxford: Blackwell Publishers, 1989), 241.

6 Yve-Alain Bois, "Perceiving Barnett Newman" in Barnett Newman: Paintings (New York: Pace Gallery, 1988), II.

7 Ibid, VI.

The allusions to Newman's zips and the way they hearken the sublime are freely acknowledged by Barnaby Furnas.[8] The faint vertical divisions running down the middle of his canvases are present in works as far ranging as *Untitled (Flood)*, 2007, *Dead Day VI*, 2008, and *Red Sea (Closing)*, 2009. On a background of pale blues, which transition from the top of these canvases into a brighter white towards the bottom, the subtly shaded zip disrupts this landscape. It forces the viewer to acknowledge the two-dimensional surfaces that are the paintings. The zips signal that we are looking at a flat image, not an illusion of a landscape.

With the paintings from the *Floods* series in particular, Furnas aggressively attacks the zips as indexes of Newman's legacy, trying to cover up and drown these linear partitions with the swelling motion of the more robust swaths of red. With *Floods*, Furnas seems to aspire to a sublime of a very different type than the Romantic representation of it or Newman's instantiation of it. Instead, Furnas's sublime asserts itself in that tension between what we see on the surface and what we know lies beyond it. It is that tension between a sense of calm and the destructive force of the flood, a tension between history (as constituted by the landscape) and the present, between the Red Sea of the Bible and the harrowing ordeal of New Orleans in 2005, between tranquility and the deluge of paint that seeks to destroy it.

A flood's poetic dovetailing of beginning and ending is manifested brilliantly in Furnas's diptych, *Red Sea (Closing)*, 2009. This work is divided into two canvases, with each one itself divided by a horizon line that juxtaposes the pale blue skyscape with a sea of red. Produced adjacent to one another, although displayed nearly two feet apart, the canvases are separated at the point where their two waves climactically connect to become something

8 Conversation with the author, August 28, 2009.

new. While the title asserts a closing of waves, there is an equal emphasis on opening in this work. The aperture between the two canvases and the planes of blue that the red stains offer up take the viewer outside of the deluge and into that fraught realm of tension that is the sublime. Opening and closing is but one of the formal and thematic polarities present in *Red Sea (Closing)*. It is reinforced by the contrast between beginning and ending, past and present, and figuration and abstraction. Those contrasts collectively function to sweep the viewer along the pours of paint into that ultimate polarity between the waves' entanglement and their eternal separation.

The tremendous size of *Red Sea (Closing)*, a nod to Old Masters' history paintings and the mythic scale of Abstract Expressionism and Color Field painting, is another effective device Furnas uses to arrest the viewer and expose the sublime. In contrast to Morris Louis (American, 1912–1962), one of the first artists to stain the unprimed canvas with acrylic so that he might get the most thoroughly integrated image of color, Furnas pours and sways his paint across the canvas so that he can best eviscerate the viewer's perceptual field. If Louis sought a purely optical viewing experience for his work, Furnas goes for the all-encompassing. To arrest one's vision is one thing; to stimulate a sensory overload is quite another.

When the viewer stands before his ultimate painting from this series, *The Whale* (2009), words fail to address the magnitude of stimulation this work provokes. *The Whale* is reminiscent of the artist's earlier series of Civil War scenes and rock concerts, only now he has rendered the spectacle in purely abstract terms. In many ways, this work is a testament to Furnas's sublime as something to which the viewer must bear witness. If earlier treatments dealt with the description of or a personal confrontation with the sublime, Furnas's work instead renders the sublime as an experience—but one that is accessible to all viewers. This is a profound departure from historical negotiations of the sublime, in that its premise is to facilitate an encounter between viewer and object and to make that confrontation as direct and visceral as possible. With this new equation of viewer and painting, the artist is no longer responsible for directing or manifesting *his* vision or experience of the sublime; instead, we arrive at a postmodern, almost democratic condition of the sublime—in which the onus falls solely on the viewer to contend with the tensions and emotions provoked by the painting. Therefore, in a work like *The Whale*, the imposing scale and the whirls of paint invite us into an experience where reason or logic is powerless. We are swept along the contours of waves into our own meditation of the sublime. Nothing is prescribed and nothing is dictated; the force of this painting and others from the *Floods* series is that Furnas facilitates a sublime experience rather than imposing his vision of it onto us.

Furnas's arsenal of scale, vibrant hues and both legendary and recent historical events are deployed with abandon to create paintings that succeed, in equal measure, at being dazzling on the surface and demanding of our thoughts. Despite all of their oppositions, these paintings suspend any sense of resolution. They are not trying to reconcile the differences between chaos and ecstasy, or an ending and a beginning. Instead, they force us to dwell, indefinitely, on such tensions formally and conceptually.

And therein lies the sublime.

Figure 1: Barnett Newman, *Vir Heroicus Sublimis*, 1950-51, oil on canvas, 7 ft 11 3/8 in x 17 ft 9 1⁄4 in. The Museum of Modern Art. Gift of Mr. and Mrs. Ben Heller

Figure 2: Barnett Newman, *Abraham*, 1949, oil on canvas, 6 ft 10 3⁄4 in x 34 1⁄2 in. The Museum of Modern Art. Philip Johnson Fund

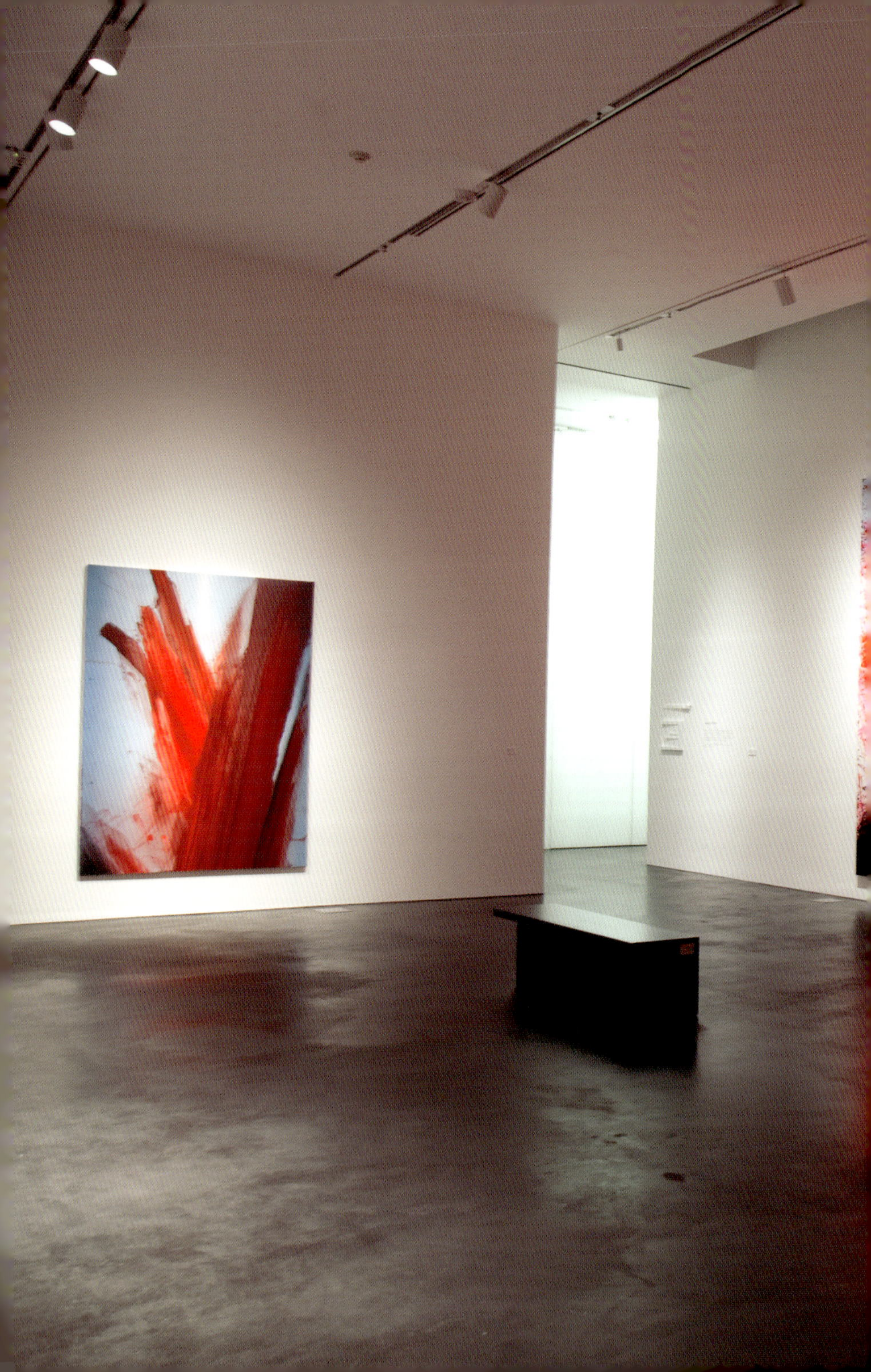

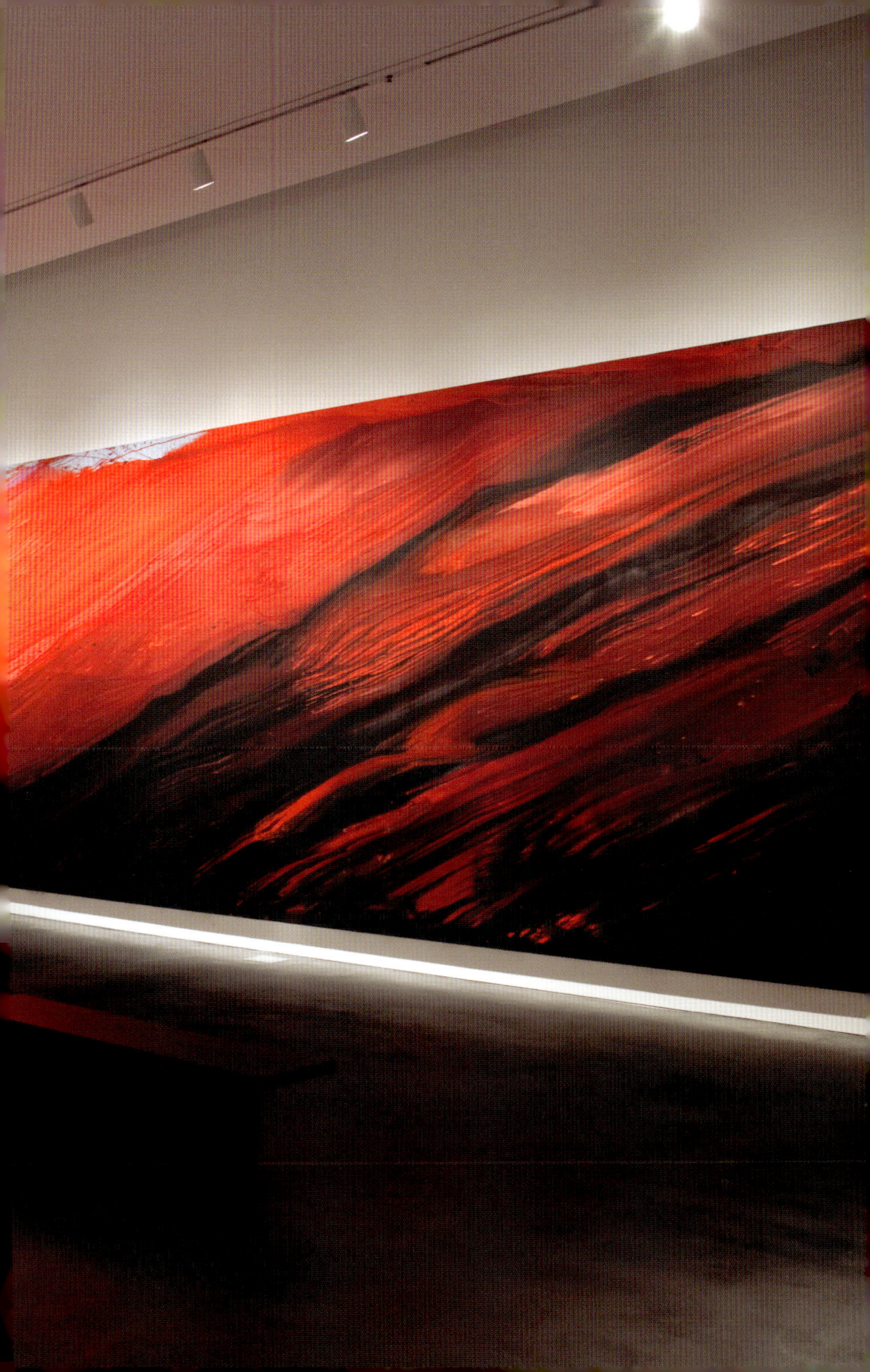

BARNABY FURNAS AND THE SOUND OF PAINT

BY ADAM LERNER

On a rare cloudy day in Denver, as sunlight dimmed and surged through light wells high overhead in the gallery, I felt something I hadn't felt in a long time. The art handlers had just finished clearing ladders and debris from the room and the massive, blood-red paintings began to glow all around us. Giant swells of red paint swept up the wall. Bright red tufts swirled like sea plants. A great red-black river gushed across an immense canvas; in another painting, a silent black ocean. I was standing with Barnaby Furnas in the midst of his *Flood* paintings, in the large gallery at MCA Denver. And the lost feeling I had recovered felt like belief.

In the past few months, art wasn't affecting me the way it had in the past. I found myself in some of the most glorious museums in the country, standing in front of my favorite works of art—and nothing swept me away. I could remember times when, standing before a work of art, I didn't want to say anything at all—because it would ruin the perfect moment I was having. I'd began to worry that I would never feel that way again.

Six months before our planned exhibition I met Barnaby for the first time, at his studio in a hip part of Brooklyn. Before the visit, I found myself wondering what he would look like. Would he affect the scruffy, vagabond look of so many other artists in his neighborhood? Or would he put on a charming, *comme des garçons* appearance of success? I met Barnaby in front of the gentrified industrial building where he kept his studio. He was wearing a polo shirt and jeans. With his short red hair and clean-shaven face, he could have been a guy with a job on his day off. What was absolutely striking about him, however, was the degree to which he didn't seem to want to *affect* anything at all. I later came to realize that that lack of affectation was his secret strength, the thing that permeates and powers all his work. When he began to talk about his paintings, he talked slowly and thoughtfully with the deliberateness of someone for whom every exchange matters. A friend of mine, who has known Barnaby for a long time, once described him as an "old soul." I was beginning to sense what my friend meant.

Standing in his large, bright studio, I asked Barnaby how he began to make his *Flood* paintings.

"In a way, I've always been making flood paintings," he explained. The *Flood* paintings came from his signature watercolors of Civil War battle scenes. He described making watercolors as "the business of creating paintings out of puddles of liquid." In order to depict the blood splatter from a bullet wound, Barnaby would splash a little water where he wanted the wound to be. "I would put a little red paint in there," he said," and the red would go *fffffffttt* and seep right through it." He conveyed a genuine interest—an artist's interest—in the physical properties of red pigment. His giant *Flood* paintings are made with essentially the same technique as his watercolors, allowing paint to flow along a more-or-less horizontal surface. What excited him most was that, in his Civil War works the red paint squirted like blood from a wound, just as in the *Flood* paintings color streamed down the large canvases like a flood. For him it was as if the paint and not the artist were making the picture. "It's like it's really happening," he said. I began to suspect a connection between his desire to be unaffected as a person and his attraction to letting paint do what it does naturally—to let paint act like paint.

In Denver, back in the gallery on the morning of the opening, Barnaby told me a story from his Quaker upbringing—a story that seemed to explain this association between his approach to the world and his approach to art.

As a child, he said, he would practice his religion in silent, unadorned rooms with clean white walls and hard benches; rooms a great deal like contemporary art galleries. "What am I supposed to do here?" eight-year-old Barnaby asked his father. "See how far away you can hear things," his father replied. "Can you follow your ears down the street, around the corner, into the 7-Eleven, down to the train station?" Barnaby took this as a lesson about being completely connected to your current situation. He later applied that lesson towards being authentic as an artist. "How close can I be to this thing I am making?" he asks, looking for his art to be as much as possible an extension of himself, without affectation.

After spending a week working on the installation with Barnaby, I got the sense that his quest for directness was a constant effort. When he told me the story about his Quaker childhood, he said, "I don't know where that memory came from. It hasn't come to me in a long time." I could see he enjoyed allowing himself to express something intuitively, even something as small as a childhood story. Early on in our work together, he told me he didn't want to be interviewed for the exhibition catalog, because all his interviews were starting to sound the same. He understood the human tendency to fall into routines, to say and do things by following past patterns, and he was constantly fighting against that propensity. This must be what it actually means for him to see how far he can hear things. He is seeing how much he can be in touch with his present condition.

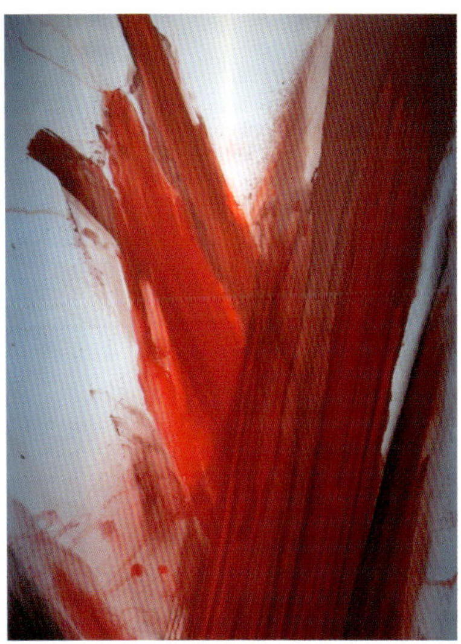

Above: *Dead Day VI*, 2008
Left: *Untitled (Flood)*, 2007

For Barnaby, being in touch is allowing accidents to happen. This is the Quaker notion of passivity, which advocates an openness to the world's contingencies, rather than a drive for perfection. Such a principle explains why he can describe his *Flood* paintings as simply "huge spill management." In the large painting he made at MCA Denver, he prepared the canvas by spraying it in advance with white and light-blue paint and then squirting it with red ink through a syringe, creating loose squiggles around the perimeter. Using large planks of wood suspended between several A-frame ladders, he propped one end of the canvas high in the air. Then, after climbing a ladder, he tossed a little bucket of swishing red and black paint down the canvas, as if discarding it. He would repeat this with bucket after bucket of paint, climbing up and down, sometimes using a brush to fling the paint out onto the surface. Using large push brooms, Barnaby and his assistants would press the paint down the canvas and constantly spray it with water. They looked like a carwash crew tackling a fire truck from all sides.

Before the painting was made, the museum staff thought they were being funny when they advertised it as being the size of a killer whale. It was originally called *The Flood*, but somehow the whale reference stuck. One morning at breakfast, someone asked Barnaby about "the whale," referring to the painting. "That's it," he said. "I'm going to call it *The Whale*." Both *The Flood* and *The Whale* have Biblical references. The new title evokes the prophet Jonah, who resisted God's orders and found himself in the belly of a great fish. More to the point, the title calls to mind Herman Melville's *Moby Dick*, an archetypal quest narrative—a story about the futility of trying to master nature. It is a perfectly fitting title for a work of art made by letting paint act like paint. Most importantly, it looks more like a whale than a flood. Unlike the other *Flood* paintings, this one appears as if something huge might be traveling though it, disturbing the waters.

I asked Barnaby about his interest in Barnett Newman, a towering figure of Postwar American painting who championed the idea of abstract painting as a spiritual endeavor. Newman believed in the sacredness of art. He thought art could connect with what he described as the "pure idea...that makes contact with the mystery—of life, of men, of nature, of the hard black chaos that is death..." Barnaby told me he wished he had such confidence. "I am more pessimistic," he said, meaning that he is not looking for the spiritual rejuvenation of society. His victories are local victories. He finds his path to the metaphysical through the physical world. That is why he doesn't talk about black chaos and death, but rather, about spill management and the *ffffffttt* of red pigment.

On the cloudy morning before the opening, standing in the gallery, I wanted to stay silent and allow the moment to happen. In art, as with everything else, there is no relying on past convictions, but only on what is happening in the room. What felt like belief was nothing more than the ability to be fully aware of sensations. It is what it feels like to hear the sound of red paint.

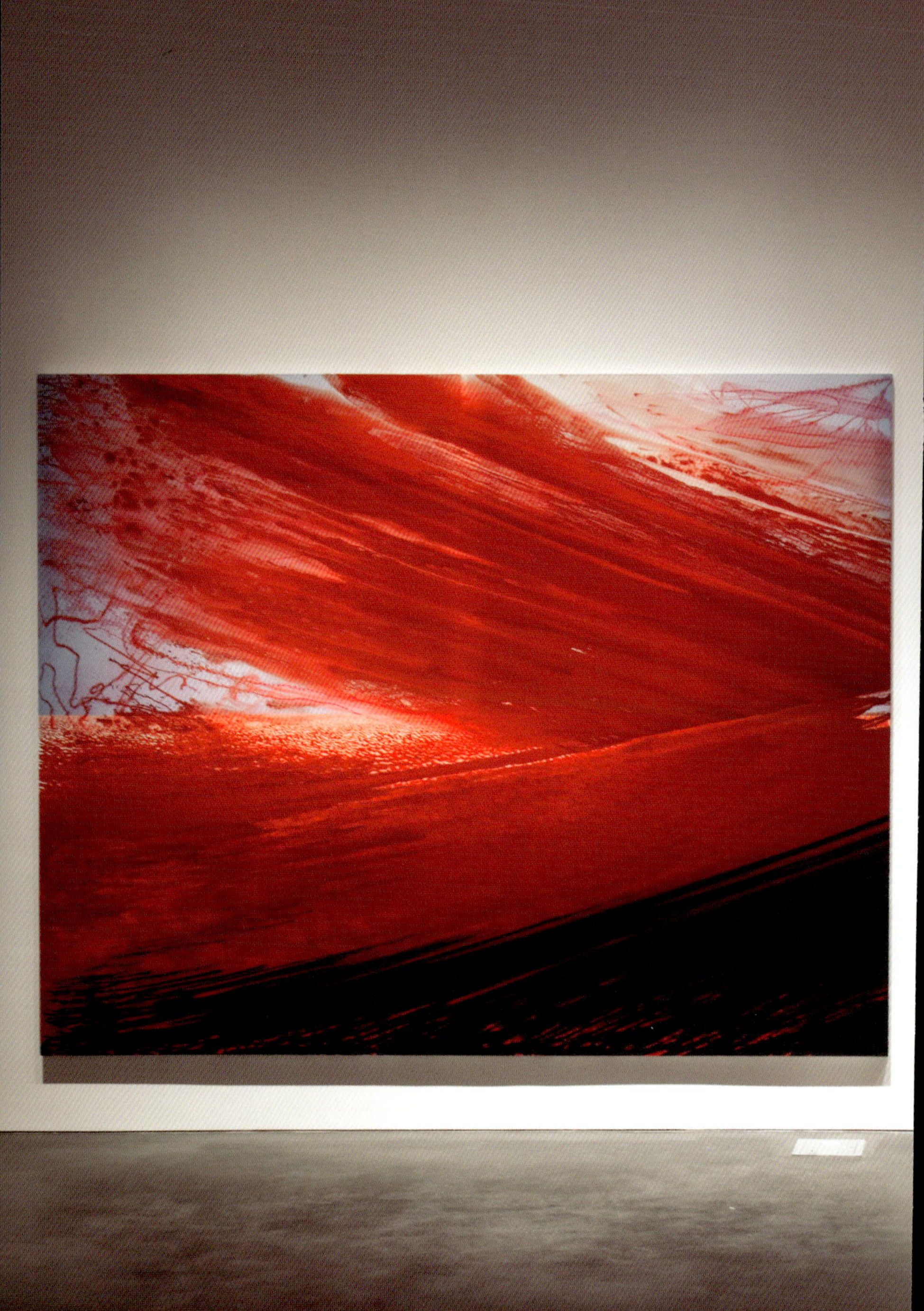

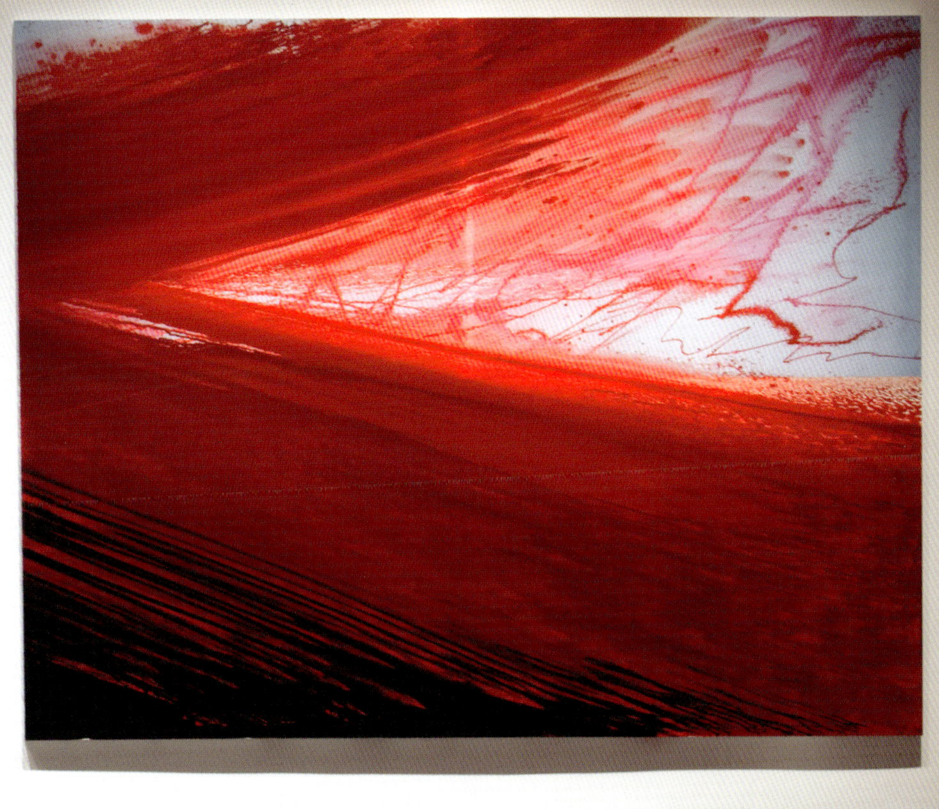

Red Sea (Closing), 2009

EXHIBITION CHECKLIST

BARNABY FURNAS *FLOODS*
MUSEUM OF CONTEMPORARY ART DENVER

September 25, 2009–January 10, 2010

Dead Day VI, 2008
Acrylic on linen
96 x 126 in
Courtesy of the artist and Marianne Boesky Gallery, New York; Modern Art, London; and Anthony Meier Fine Art, San Francisco

Red Sea (Closing), 2009
Acrylic, water dispersed pigments and dye on linen
Diptych, each: 102 x 132 in
Courtesy of the artist and Marianne Boesky Gallery, New York; Modern Art, London; and Anthony Meier Fine Art, San Francisco

The Whale, 2009
Acrylic, water dispersed pigments and dye on linen
150 x 360 in
Courtesy of the artist and Marianne Boesky Gallery, New York; Modern Art, London; and Anthony Meier Fine Art, San Francisco

Untitled (Flood), 2007
Urethane, dye and dispersed pigment on linen
96 x 72 in
Private Collection, Los Angeles

CURRICULAE VITAE

BARNABY FURNAS

Biography

Born 1973, Philadelphia

Education

2000

Columbia University, New York, MFA

1995

School of Visual Arts, New York, BFA

Solo Exhibitions

2011

Modern Art Museum of Fort Worth, Texas

2009

Anthony Meier, San Francisco

Museum of Contemporary Art Denver

2008

"Closed Loop," Marianne Boesky Gallery, New York

Stuart Shave/Modern Art, London

2007

"Focus: Barnaby Furnas," Modern Art Museum of Fort Worth, Texas

2006

Marianne Boesky Gallery, New York

Anthony Meier Fine Art, San Francisco

2005

BALTIC Centre for Contemporary Art, Gateshead, UK (catalogue)

Lever House, New York

2004

Modern Art Inc., London

2003

Marianne Boesky Gallery, New York

2002

Marianne Boesky Gallery, New York

Group Exhibitions

2009

"Something About Mary," The Metropolitan Opera, New York, September 17, 2009–January 31, 2010

"The Audio Show," Friedrich Petzel Gallery, New York

White Space Beijing DOMUS COLLECTION NEW YORK | BEIJING

2008

"WALL ROCKETS: Contemporary Artists and Ed Ruscha," The FLAG Art Foundation, New York

"The Old, Weird America," Contemporary Arts Museum Houston, curated by Toby Kamps, Travels to DeCordova, Lincoln, Mass.; Frye Art Museum, Seattle

"You dig the tunnel; I'll hide the soil," White Cube Hoxton and Shoreditch Town Hall, London, curated by Harland Miller

"Blown Away," Krannert Art Museum and Kinkead Pavilion, Champaign, Ill., curated by Ginger Gregg Duggan and Judith Hoos Fox

"Under Pain of Death," Austrian Cultural Forum New York, curated by Kunsthalle Wien (Gerald Matt, Ilse Lafer) and Abraham Orden

2007

"True Romance. Allegories of Love from the Renaissance to the Present," Kunsthalle Wien, Austria

"The Fractured Figure," Deste Foundation, Athens

"Dream and Trauma: Works from the Dakis Joannou Collection, Athens," Kunsthalle Wien and Museum Moderner Kunst Stiftung Ludwig, Vienna

"Art in America: Now," Museum of Contemporary Art, Shanghai, China–contemporary portion of "Art in America: 300 Years of Innovation," organized by the Guggenheim Museum

Traveling exhibition: Pushkin Museum of Fine Arts, Moscow; Guggenheim Bilbao, Spain

"Between Two Deaths," Zentrum fuer Kunst und Medientechnologie, Karlsruhe, Germany

"The Old, Weird America," Contemporary Arts Center, Cincinnatti

"Counterparts: Contemporary Painters and their Influences," Contemporary Art Center of Virginia, Virginia Beach (catalogue)

2006

"Surrealism: Then and Now," Paul Kasmin Gallery, New York

"USA Today," The Royal Academy of Arts, in collaboration with the Saatchi Gallery, London

"Nightmares of Summer," Marvelli Gallery, New York, curated by George Robertson

"Imagination Becomes Reality, Part IV: Borrowed Images," Sammlung Goetz, Munich, travels to Museum for Neue Kunst, Karlsruhe

2005

"PILLish: Harsh Realities and Gorgeous Destinations," Museum of Contemporary Art Denver

2004

"Seeing Other People," Marianne Boesky Gallery, New York

"179 Annual: An Invitational Exhibition of Contemporary Art," National Academy of Design, New York (catalogue)

"2004 Whitney Biennial," Whitney Museum of American Art, New York

"Watercolor Worlds," Dorsky Gallery, Long Island City, New York

"Beginning Here: 101 Ways," School of Visual Arts, Visual Arts Gallery, New York

2003

"Go Johnny Go," Kunsthalle Wien, Austria

"War (What Is It Good For?)," Museum of Contemporary Art, Chicago

"Funny Papers: Cartoons and Contemporary Drawing," Daniel Weinberg Gallery, Los Angeles

"Transnational Monster League," Derek Eller Gallery, New York, curated by Banks Violette

"Drawings," Metro Pictures, New York

2002

"Officina Americana," Galleria d'Arte Moderna, Bologna, Italy

"The Fourth Annual Altoids Curiously Strong Collection," Los Angeles Contemporary Exhibition, Los Angeles

2001

Marianne Boesky Gallery, New York

"All American," Bellwether, Brooklyn

2000

"Collector's Choice," Exit Art, New York

"Project Room," Artist's Space, New York

Marianne Boesky Gallery, New York

"@," P.P.O.W. Gallery, New York, curated by Jason Murison

1999

"All Terrain," Freidrich Petzel Gallery, New York

"Urban Romantics," Lombard Fried Gallery, New York

Bibliography

2007

Mendelsohn, Adam E. "Barnaby Furnas," Heyoka Magazine, Volume 7, Spring 2007

Bourbon, Matthew. "Barnaby Furnas," Artforum.com, http://artforum.com/picks/section=us#id15289, May 2007

Karnes, Andrea "Focus: Barnaby Furnas," The Modern Art Museum, Fort Worth (brochure)

2006

Stevens, Mark and Karen Rosenberg, "Art," New York Magazine, December 18, 2006, p. 66-68, ill.

Peers, Alexandra. "Auctions: Contemporary Grows Up," New York Magazine, November 6, 2006, p. 97, ill.

Douglas, Sarah. "Fiery Furnas," Art + Auction, November 2006, p. 210

Nally, Whitney M. "Star Search," W Magazine, November 2006, p. 192-193

Kastner, Jeffrey. "Art In Review," The New York Times, October 13, 2006, p. E36

Mendelsohn, Adam E. "Barnaby Furnas," Time Out New York, October 12-18, 2006, p. 71, ill.

Kazakina, Katya. "Furnas's Flood, Opie's Cities, McCracken's Columns: Chelsea Art," Bloomberg.com, October 4, 2006

Alemani, Cecilia. "Barnaby Furnas," Artforum.com, October 2006, http://www.artforum.com/picks/section=nyc#picks11797

Rousseau, Bryant. "My Collection: Stavros Merjos," Art Info, October 2, 2006, ill.

_____. Review, The New Yorker, October 9, 2006, p. 15

Miller, Leigh Anne. "Met Opera Enlists Art Stars," Art In America, October 2006, p. 41-42, ill.

Cohen, David. "Apocalypse Now," The New York Sun, September 28, 2006

_____ "Wandering Eye," Nylon Newsletter, September 21, 2006

Rosenberg, Karen. "Art," New York Magazine, September 4-11, 2006, p. 69, ill.

LeBlanc, Marc. "Barnaby Furnas," Beautiful/Decay, September 2006, pp. 60-66

Kazanjian, Dodie. "Paging Picasso," Vogue, September 2006, pp. 670-677

Egan, Maura. "Splash Art," Departures Magazine, September 2006, pp. 142-144

Van De Walle, Mark. "Patriotic Gore," Men's Vogue, September 2006

Vogel, Carol. "Where Bel Canto Meets Paintbrush," The New York Times, August 15, 2006, pp. E1 & E5

Tomkins, Calvin. "The Creative Life: The Pour," The New Yorker, March 13, 2006, pp. 32-34

2004

Kunitz, Daniel. "Institutional Exhibitionism," The New York Sun, May 6, 2004

_____. "Amuseum: The Funhouse Effect in the Whitney Biennial," Gallery & Studio, April/May 2004

Sozanski, Edward J. "A view from the front line," The Philadelphia Inquirer, March 14, 2004

Nichols, Matthew Guy. Review, Art In America, February 2004

Image printed, Harper's, February 2004

2003

Kastner, Jeffrey. Review, Artforum, November 2003

Vogel, Carol. "More Eyes on the Mix For Whitney Biennial," The New York Times, October 27, 2003

Reed, John. Review, Time Out New York, October 2-9, 2003

Mar, Alex. Review, The New York Sun, October 2, 2003

Dumenco, Simon. Review, New York Magazine, September 2003

Mar, Alex. Review, The New York Sun, April 24, 2003

2002

Firstenberg, Lauri. Flash Art, November–December 2002

Eleey, Peter. Review, Frieze, September 2002

Kantor, Jordan. Review, Artforum, September 2002

Levin, Kim. "Shortlist: Art," Village Voice, May 8, 2002, p. 90

Johnson, Ken. "Art in Review: Barnaby Furnas," The New York Times, May 3, 2002, E39

Bovee, Katherine. "The New Perversion," March Magazine, 2002

2001

Cotter, Holland. "All American," The New York Times, August 3, 2001

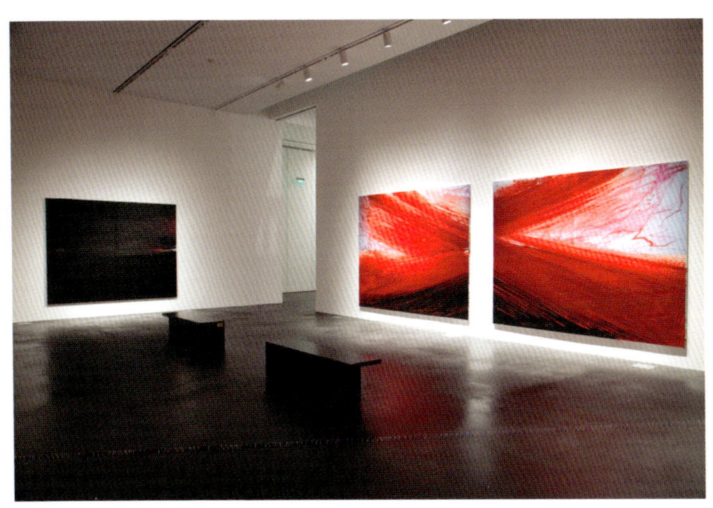

Acknowledgments

The exhibition Barnaby Furnas *Floods* was sponsored in part by Scott Miller & Tim Gill and MCA Denver's Director's Vision Society.

I am immensely grateful to Barnaby for partnering with MCA Denver to create this painting, exhibition and catalog. His generosity of spirit was an enormous gift to our institution and our city. And I cannot thank Karl Kister enough for the brilliant suggestion of exhibiting Barnaby's flood paintings. A heartfelt thanks to the people who did so much to make the artist and his guests feel welcome: Ellen Bruss & Mark Falcone, Philae Dominick, David Scanavino, and Emily Sinclair & Jay Kenney. MCA Denver acknowledges Marianne Boesky Gallery in New York, Modern Art in London and Anthony Meier Fine Art in San Francisco. I am especially grateful to Marianne, whom it was such a pleasure to get to know through this process. Thank you to Tony Meier for his generous hospitality. Thank you to Nora Burnett Abrams for her hard work and brain power. I want to thank the MCA Denver staff and volunteers who worked tirelessly to make this exhibition possible. Thanks to Jared Preston for his faithful assistance with the painting and installation and Jane Panetta for her help with image rights. And, finally, a special thank you to the 1,000+ people of Denver who came out to support the artist at his opening reception.

– A.L.

About the Authors

Nora Burnett Abrams, adjunct curator at the MCA Denver, is a PhD candidate at the Institute of Fine Arts at New York University. She was a curatorial assistant at The Metropolitan Museum of Art and at the Grey Art Gallery, NYU's fine arts museum, where she held a curatorial fellowship. She is a graduate of Stanford University and holds a master's degree in modern art from Columbia University.

Adam Lerner is the Director of the Museum of Contemporary Art Denver and Chief Animator in the Department of Structures and Fictions.

Published 2009

Published in conjunction with the exhibition Barnaby Furnas *Floods*
September 25, 2009–January 10, 2010

Designed by Michele Bury
Barnaby Furnas photographs by Grant Leighton
Avenir (1988) Typeface by Adrian Frutiger

Printed by Sprint Press, Denver, CO

Bound by Roswell Bookbinding, Phoenix, AZ

Edition of 2000

ISBN 1-931867-16-X
ISBN13 978-1-931867-16-0

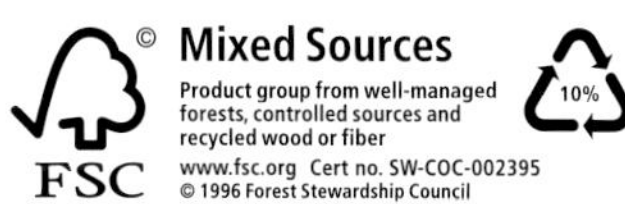